A GREAT WEEKEND IN

# BARCELONA

# A GREAT WEEKEND IN BARCELONA

*The spellbinding Catalan capital*

Barcelona is a city of contrasts set between the mountains and the sea, a tireless reveller by night and hard-working by day, fervently European yet fiercely Catalan. *Seny* – common sense – and *rauxa* – a touch of madness – make it fluctuate between tradition and innovation. Loyal to its past, but ever reaching out towards new galaxies, it combines imagination with a sharp nose for business.

*'It isn't possible to talk of one Barcelona, because Barcelona is made up of several distinct interwoven elements. Archaeologists ought to know why eternal cities are made up of archaeological layers, as if the place they chose for their existence was the result of a vague yet inevitable plan,'* observed Manuel Vázquez Montalbán in his *Barcelonas.* Notable travellers of the thirties, such as Joseph Kessel, and those associated with the Civil War, like George Orwell and Ernest Hemingway,

wouldn't recognise the port areas of the city today. The slogan of the nineties, 'Make Barcelona Beautiful' inspired architectural projects galore, which have transformed this former legendary stronghold of resistance to Francoism. With the arrival of the Olympic Games in 1992, Barcelona decided to buck up its ideas and with envigorating enthusiasm has given several of its old quarters a creative and well thought-out face-lift.

The capital of Catalonia burst into frenzied action and museums, shops, restaurants, bars and galleries flourished. Modernity, creativity and the Catalan identity blended to produce a visual feast. From old fashioned town houses to the latest bars and from the old-fashioned charm of a cabaret in the Barrio Chino to the stunts of an acrobat on La Rambla, you will find yourself in the middle of a forward-looking city, full of life and colour, but also proud of its past. Indeed, the people of Barcelona take their roots very seriously. Holidays and festivals follow on one from another in a whirlwind of tradition. Southern European

in terms of their fierce pride and attachment to tradition, northern European in terms of their work ethic and business acumen, Catalans cultivate their identity as others cultivate their prize blooms, jealously and with care.

Wander through the labyrinth of narrow streets and come across a delightful shaded patio concealing a collection of Picassos, or sit on the terrace of the Plaça del Pi and sip a *horchata* to the sound of an

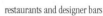

amateur saxophone player. If you like to sample the food of a new city as well as its atmosphere, try La Boqueria, the covered market situated on La Rambla, which is a riot of delicious smells and colour and everything that a mediterranean market should be. Try some dried fruit and nuts for a snack and then head for the port and the revitalised shoreline of Barceloneta. Lined with trendy

restaurants and designer bars you can sample *copas* and *tapas* and watch families out for their Sunday afternoon consitutionals. It's a city that rarely sleeps. Catalans say with a superior air, that siestas are for Andalucians. Barcelona nights are neon-lit, retro, rococo, sequined or high-tech. Adopt the Catalan mentality of work hard and play hard, and embark on a round of the bars. You'll need a lot of stamina and the ability to stay awake well into the small hours. The people of Barcelona certainly know how to enjoy life. However, whether you're a party animal or more inclined to stroll around admiring the architecture, you'll just love your weekend in Barcelona.

# How to get there

The ideal seasons for visiting Barcelona are the spring and autumn. From March onwards, you'll start to encounter the heat, but be on the lookout for frequent showers around Easter. Several big religious festivals light up the streets between March and June.

## HOW TO GET THERE

For a great weekend in Barcelona, the best way to get there is probably by plane. From the UK and Ireland, the flight takes approximately two and a half hours. From the USA, Canada and Australasia, it is, of course, considerably longer and invariably requires a stopover, though there are some direct flights (see details below). From continental Europe, the train is also an option, though probably only if you're going for more than a couple of days, since it might require a night on board. The train journey from the UK could take up to 30 hours (see p.6).

## WHEN TO GO

Temperatures can soar to as high as 37°C/99°F in July and August, so avoid the summer months if you can't stand the heat and crowds of tourists. However, cultural activity is at its height in July, with the Greek theatre staging musical entertainment and plays and bringing together foreign and Catalan companies. From 15 August for two weeks, Barcelona is the centre for the unique traditional celebrations of Gràcia (see p. 16). September and October remain sunny and the Diada, the national holiday on 11 September, is very enjoyable. If you do decide to go at the end of autumn or in winter, don't worry about the cold as the climate is still mild at that time of year, though temperatures can fall to below 7°C/45°F at night in February. You could also join in the celebrations at Christmas and New Year (see p. 14). On 5th/6th January the Festa del Reis takes place – the Festival of the Three Kings, or the Three Wise Men, when children traditionally receive their presents.

## FLIGHTS FROM THE UK

**British Airways**
www.british-airways.com
☎ 0345 222 111
Regular flights to Barcelona –
call for schedules.

**Virgin Express**
☎ 020 7744 0004
www.virgin-express.com
Has flights from Heathrow,
Stansted and Gatwick – all of
which go via Brussels.

**Iberia**
☎ 0345 341 341
www.iberia.com
Has 3 flights a day from
Heathrow to Barcelona and
one per day from Manchester.

**Easyjet**
☎ 0870 6000 000
www.easyjet.com
Offer cheaper 'no-frills' flights
to Barcelona. Book as far as
possible in advance for the
bargain fares.

**Debonair**
☎ 0541 500 300
www.debonair.co.uk
Flights from Liverpool
and London.

## FROM IRELAND

**British Airways**
☎ 1-800-626-747
www.british-airways.com
Offer flights from Shannon,
Cork, and Dublin to
Barcelona via London
Gatwick.

**Iberia**
☎ 01-407-3017
www.iberia.com
Offer one direct flight per day
from Dublin to Barcelona.
Flights from other cities in
Ireland go via Dublin.

## FROM THE USA AND CANADA

**British Airways**
☎ 1-800-AIRWAYS
www.british-airways.com
Daily flights via London from
all over the USA and Canada.

**Delta**
☎ 1-800-241-241
www.delta-air.com
Has some direct flights to
Barcelona via JFK. Call for
more information.

---

### BUDGET

Barcelona is no longer
a particularly cheap
destination. Spain, like
Italy, is nowadays as
expensive as any other
European country. The
peseta is quite strong and
hotel prices have risen
quite considerably in recent
years and of course prices
in the city inevitably tend
to be higher than in the
smaller towns.

For two people, you
should consider budgeting
along the lines of 25,000-
33,000 ptas a day for good-
class accommodation,
meals and outings.
Above all, when making
your hotel reservations,
make sure you ask for
the *'fin de semana'* price
(see p.68).

You can expect to pay
3,000 to 6,000 ptas for a
meal, from 800 to 1,000
ptas for a museum ticket,
125 ptas for a bus ticket,
300 to 600 ptas for a
non-alcoholic drink,
1,000 to 2,000 ptas for a
disco, 2,500 ptas for a
concert seat, and up
to 185 ptas to send
a postcard to
Australia.

**Iberia**
☎ 1-800-772-4642
www.iberia.com
Offer direct flights – call for
more information.

## FROM AUSTRALIA AND NEW ZEALAND

There are no direct flights to
Barcelona from Australia and
New Zealand, but it's possible
to stop over in other European
cities, such as London, en
route. Check with your travel
agent for flight details or try
looking on the web.

## BY TRAIN

Most international trains
arrive in Barcelona at the
Estació de França (metro
Barceloneta). If you're
arriving in Barcelona from
within Spain, you'll arrive at
Estació Sants (metro Sants
Estació). It's a long journey
from the UK or Ireland and
you'll need to allow between
20 and 30 hours! If you do
decide to take the train, your
trip will, of course, include
crossing the English Channel,

which you can do by ferry
or by taking the Eurostar
(☎ 0990 186 186) to Paris.
From there you could take
the Trenhotel ('hotel train'),
an overnight service offering

sleeper accommodation.
The journey takes just over
12 hours and you should
ask at one of the rail
companies listed about
this service.

### LOCAL AND FOREIGN CURRENCY

The national currency is
the peseta. You'll come
across it in 10,000, 5,000,
2,000 and 1,000 peseta
notes and 500, 200, 100, 50,
25, 10, 5 (commonly known
as a *duro)* and 1 peseta
coins.

The euro was launched in
Spain on 1 January 1999
but euro coins and notes
won't be in use until 1
January 2002. The peseta
will continue alongside it
until 1 July 2002, when it
will be replaced by a euro
worth about 165ptas.

If you change any money
before you go, don't carry

too much cash around
with you – pickpocketing
is rife and the thieves are
amazingly efficient. Take a
bum-bag or money-belt
with you to keep your
credit card and wallet in
safely. Leave documents,
passports, plane tickets
and money in the hotel
safe.

There are plenty of cash
machines in the city and
you'll be able to withdraw
cash easily using a credit
card. If you need to carry
large sums of money
around with you, it's better
to take traveller's cheques.

**European Rail**
☎ 020 7387 0444 (UK)
www.europeanrail.co.uk

**The International Rail Centre**
☎ 0990 848 848 (UK)
Or ask your travel agent for more information. If you need information about rail services within Spain, call the national rail operator RENFE on
☎ 93 490 02 02 (domestic), or ☎ 93 490 11 22 (international).

## BY COACH

The journey by coach can take up to a whole day, so it isn't really an option for just a weekend. However, you might consider it if you're going for a slightly longer break. From the UK there are regular bus services to Spain. Eurolines (☎ 0990 143 219) has services to Barcelona. Ask at major travel agencies, or visit their website at www.eurolines.co.uk for more

information. Within Barcelona, buses usually arrive at Estació del Nord (metro Arc de Triomf), though some international buses arrive at Estació de Sants.

**Estació del Nord**
☎ 93 265 65 08.

**Estació de Sants**
☎ 93 490 04 00.

## FROM THE AIRPORT TO THE CITY CENTRE
The airport of Prat, 12km/7 miles south of Barcelona, is linked to the city by way of the Castelldefels motorway. There are various ways for you to get to the centre.

### BY TRAIN
From 6am to 10pm, it takes 25 minutes to get to the Sants and Plaça de Catalunya station, with departures every half-hour. Tickets cost 350 ptas.

### BY AIRPORT BUS
From 6.30am to 11pm, a bus leaves every quarter of an hour for the Plaça de Catalunya, stopping at the Plaça d'Espanya and Plaça de la Universitat. Tickets cost 475 ptas and the journey takes half an hour.

### BY TAXI
For a cost of 2,500 ptas, you can reach the city centre in half an hour.

**Airport information**
☎ 93 298 38 38.

**Transport information**
☎ 93 412 00 00.

## CUSTOMS
You can take up to 800 cigarettes, 60 litres of wine and 10 litres of spirits into Spain with you. You can also import some foodstuffs. In June 1999 duty-free allowances were abolished between EU countries, but if you enter Spain from a non-EU country you can bring in 200 cigarettes, 1 litre of wine, 1 litre of spirits and 50cl of perfume duty-free.

## FORMALITIES
EU-citizens only require an identity card or passport. Citizens of the USA, Canada, Australia and New Zealand don't require a visa, just a passport. Foreign embassies are all located in Madrid.

**UK**
☎ 91 319 02 00
Calle de Fernando el Santo

### LOCAL TIME
Spain is one hour ahead of GMT, except from the end of March to the end of September, when it's 2 hours. To sample the true Catalan lifestyle, you really need to know the times of meals. Lunch is usually between 1.30pm and 2pm, and dinner is eaten very late, at 10pm. Shops are generally shut between 2pm and 4pm, (see p.82), and banks and museums are generally open from 10am to 2pm and closed in the afternoon (the exceptions being the Miró and Tapiès foundations and the Picasso museum, see p.38). The central post office is open from 8am to 10pm (see p. 32), and bars don't begin to buzz until 1am in the morning (p 112), so serious clubbers will need a good lie-in to prepare for the night ahead.

## Useful addresses and information

### Spanish Tourist Offices worldwide

**UK & Ireland**
22-23 Manchester Square
London
W1M 5AP
☎ 020 7486 8077

**USA**
666, 5th Avenue
35th floor
New York
NY 10103
☎ 212 265 8822

8383 Wilshire Blvd
Beverly Hills
Los Angeles
CA 90211
☎ 213 658 7188

845 North Michigan Avenue
Chicago
IL 60611
☎ 312 642 1992

1221 Brickell Avenue
Suite 1850
Miami
FL 33131
☎ 305 358 1992

**Australia and New Zealand**
c/o Spanish Tour
Promotions
178 Collins Street
Melbourne
☎ 03 9650 737

(For tourist offices in Barcelona, see page 33).

### Websites

Some good websites with plenty of tourist information are:
**www.tourspain.es**
**www.okspain.org**
Both offer detailed practical information on the whole of Spain. The Tourspain site also offers detailed information on Barcelona, so check them out before you go.
If you want to find out more while you're away, you can use the Internet for half an hour for 600 ptas at:
**Insolit**
Maremagnum, local 111
(C3) ☎ 93 225 81 78
(see p. 117).

**USA**
☎ 91 587 22 00
Calle de Serrano, 75

**Canada**
☎ 91 431 43 00
Calle de Nuñde Balbao, 35

**Australia**
☎ 91 431 43 00
Plaza del Descubridor
Diego de Ordás 3-2,
Edificio Santa Engracia, 120

**New Zealand**
☎ 91 523 02 26
Plaza de la Lealtad, 2

### Health & Insurance

No vaccinations are needed. EU citizens are entitled to basic health care in case of illness or accident. The *Barcelona Centro Medico* is responsible for helping foreign patients.

**Barcelona Centro Medico**
Avinguda Diagonal 437,
☎ 93 414 06 43 (24hrs)
☎ 93 290 68 59.
Obtain an E111 form (available from UK post offices) and take out travel insurance to cover theft. Paying for your trip by credit card may cover you for some medical assistance and lost luggage.

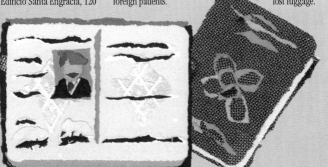

# A TASTE OF THE SUN AND THE MOUNTAINS

Like the country itself, Catalan cuisine has an authentic rustic flavour. The contrasting tastes of the Pyrenees and Mediterranean are combined in simple delicious dishes. Plain ingredients are simmered to conjure up substantial, nourishing fare, such as wild rabbit with prawns, beef stew with haricot beans, partridge with cabbage, cod with ratatouille, charcoal grilled snails with boletus mushrooms and many more designed to tempt the appetite with all the mouth-watering aromas of Catalonia.

## THE BASIC INGREDIENTS: SAUCES AND *PA AMB TOMÀQUET*

Catalan cuisine is generally prepared with olive oil or lard and uses a few basic sauces. *Picada* is made from almonds, garlic, pine nuts, walnuts, hazelnuts, oil, stale bread, warm water and chopped parsley ground in a mortar. *Sofregit* is made from finely-chopped fried onions and tomato. *Samfain* is a

ratatouille made from peppers, aubergines, tomatoes and sometimes onions. *Ailloli* contains just garlic, oil and salt. Simple but irresistible *pa amb tomàquet* (bread and tomatoes) accompanies meals. It consists of a slice of toast rubbed with raw tomato and sprinkled with salt and a dash of olive oil (at the **Casa Leopoldo**).

## A TASTE OF THE SUN IN WINTER

*Escudella i carn d'olla* is a tasty stew made from beef, pig's ears and trotters, poultry, lamb, black and white *botifares* sausages, cabbage, celery, carrots, turnips, potatoes and haricot beans. To these are added *pilota*, a mixture of minced pork and veal combined with white breadcrumbs, eggs and spices. It's a typical regional dish that's prepared on cold days and always served in the Christmas season.

## MEDITERRANEAN FLAVOURS

With one foot in the country and the other on the coast, Catalans appreciate the produce of both the mountains and the Mediterranean. Aperitifs are served with shellfish *tapas* which are prepared with *tellines* and razor-shells (razor clams), fried red mullet and glass-eels, and grilled octopus and squid (at **Cal Pep**). Or you can try *suquet de peix*, Costa Brava-style bouillabaisse, sea bream

## CATALAN COOKING UTENSILS

If you long to emulate the locals in their cuisine, here are a few utensils you'll need to make tasty Catalan dishes successfully, together with the names of the shops where you can buy them. *Paella* dishes can be found at **Targa**, while *olles*, the traditional olive and sand-coloured terracotta cooking pots, salamander irons and ramekins for *crema catalana* (crème brûlée), and *porròs*, glass jugs with long spouts for drinking the local Pénédès white wine, can all be found at **Caixa de Fang** (see p. 97). Enjoy!

in a salt crust, *daurada a la sal*, and *arros negre*, black rice in cuttlefish ink, at **Set Portes** or in the shade of a vine on the Tibidabo hill (see p. 61).

branches and served with *ailloli*. In winter, the traditional *calçotada* unites family and friends round *calçots a la brasa*, leeks grilled over a wood fire, served with a sauce whose recipe is a closely-guarded secret (at **Rancho Grande**). *Butifarra negra*, or black pudding, is made from lean pork mixed with pig's blood. *Butifarra de l'Empordà* is sweetened and flavoured with lemon peel and cinnamon using a recipe that dates back to the Middle Ages.

## TEMPTING DESSERTS

Of all the many mouth-watering desserts — crisp biscuits, spiced cakes and fromage blanc coated with honey and almonds — there's one, *crema catalana* or *cremada*, that's irresistibly smooth (at **Viader**). This delicious crème brûlée flavoured with cinnamon is served with a misty glass of chilled *cava*. This local champagne is a speciality of the village of Sant Sadurni d'Anoia, where you can visit the Codorniù cellars in their magnificent *Modernista* setting.

## THROUGHOUT THE YEAR

Catalonia is generous with its produce in every season and the Catalans are especially fond of *cargolades*, traditional country dishes made from snails and meat grilled on vine

## *COPAS, TAPAS* AND THE REST

Barcelona is a city of cafés and bars. Some of them have already become the stuff of legend – Le Suizo, l'Oro del Rin and La Luna – while others are boldly avant-garde. In a city which has such a variety of disctricts, each with its own distinctive character, you'll come across bars decorated with bric-a-brac, home-made distilleries with closely guarded secrets and *tapas* bars with ancient counters worn smooth by generations. There is something to suit everyone, from elderly domino players and veterans reliving past glories to the energetic and exuberant young.

### ENTERTAINING CATALAN-STYLE

Catalans don't readily invite people to their homes. As in many Mediterranean countries, people socialise in the street. An invitation *anar de tasca* or *ir de tapas* is seen as a mark of trust. You spend the evening going from bar to bar, never to get drunk but more to meet informally over tempting snacks and a glass of the local wine.

### HOT AND SPICY

The word *tapas* is said to come from the covers that used to be placed over glasses of wine to stop flies falling in (*tapar* means to close or stop). Once a piece of ham or cheese had been placed on the top it was only a short step towards creating the *tapas* we know today. The *tapas* menu is hugely varied, from *escalivada*, pickled aubergines and peppers in olive oil, to fried octopus, and from anchovies to the *embotits* (sausages and hams) of the Pyrenees. *Fuets*, dry sausages, sausage with black pepper and *pernil serrano*, a local ham, will all be on the menu.

### *TAPAS* ETIQUETTE

The *tapas* tradition is most firmly rooted in Andalusia and the Basque Country and takes a slightly different form in Catalonia. You order *a la barra* (at the bar), *de raciòn* or *media raciòn* (a portion or half-portion) a little before dinner time (see p. 8), and avoid raising your voice to distinguish yourself from Andalusians, whom the Catalans consider far too noisy. People usually pay for their own drinks, though you can also buy a round of course, if you would like to do so.

### CHIRINGUITO AND BODEGA

A *bodega* is a wine bar or inn that's sometimes decorated with casks and barrels to add local colour. Drinks are served to order and it isn't uncommon for the wine list to feature a selection of cold meats.

The *Can* or *Casa* offers home cooking, with produce fresh from the market simmering on the stove. The seafront *chiringuito* is a fishermen's restaurant, while the *fonda* is an inn where you eat whatever's in the pot. *Granjas* make delicious sweets from farm and dairy produce, while *horchaterias* specialise in barley water flavoured with almonds or tiger nuts, *horchata de chufa*.

### ONLY HERE

Anything is possible in a Barcelona bar, especially games like *Manilla*, Catalan tarot or the card game *subhastat*, or *belote*. Old men from the locality play the afternoon away using chickpeas or grains of corn as counters. Elsewhere there are fruit machines to lead you astray, though the **Nick Havanna** bar has installed a book vending machine to salve your conscience. The **Canodrom Pavello bar**, with its dilapidated decor, is host to the gamblers from the nearby greyhound track. With French billiards already on offer at the **Velòdrom**, darts available elsewhere and Internet cafés up and running, the latest to open its doors, the **Arquer**, has invented *copas y flechas* – you can have a drink

## THE MARSELLA AND FRANCO'S DICTATORSHIP

The **Marsella's** decor hasn't changed since it was founded in 1820 by a native of Marseilles as a place to drink absinthe. Since the turn of the century the Lamiel family have presided here. During the fascist dictatorship, singing and meetings were strictly forbidden in the bar, and the writing on the tarnished mirrors still reads *'està prohibido cantar'*. If this somewhat decadent setting appeals to you, you can also have your cards read by a tarot expert.

while brushing up your archery for 1,200 ptas, and win hearts into the bargain by playing Robin Hood!

# RELIGIOUS FESTIVALS AND TRADITIONS

Throughout the year, religious festivals and traditions turn the city into an open-air theatre. Popular culture is still very much alive, delighting crowds of onlookers with processions of papier-mâché giants. With Fellini-style cross-dressing at carnival time, interminable dancing of *sardanas* (see p.17) and amazing balancing acts by *castellers* (see p. 6), these festivals are a very lively sight indeed. Each celebration is accompanied by special sweets and cakes and the shop windows are full of colour. Barcelona is a festive city throughout the year.

## DECEMBER

From 13 December onwards, Santa Llucia's (St Lucy's) Day, the cathedral square is covered with stalls on which tinsel, baubels, beads and ribbons make you dream of Christmas. The crib figures are given a place of honour, displayed in a setting of bark and moss, but the presence of the *caganer* – a typical Catalan figure of a shepherd relieving himself – is a big surprise. He's supposed to be fertilising the ground and is thus a fertility symbol (you can buy crib figures at **Rosés**, see p. 90).

## JANUARY

To celebrate New Year' Eve, family and friends gather to eat the *postre del music* (musician's dessert) made of honey, dried fruit and *matò* (curdled milk). On the stroke of midnight, everyone eats twelve grapes for good luck in time with the chimes. During the night of 5th to 6th January small children leave *turróns* and dried fruit for the Wise Men, along with bread and water for the camels. These same Wise Men disembark at the port for the *cabalgata De los Reyes Magos* (the Procession of the Three Wise Men). This is the most magical time of all for the children. They have already written out their lists of longed-for presents and treats, having handed them in to one of the pages who were in the city a few days earlier. The Wise Men now hand out the presents, but naughty children are only given a lump of coal.

## FEBRUARY

From Shrove Tuesday to Ash Wednesday the *Carnestoltes*, carnival celebrations, which were banned for a long time under Franco, take place.

On the last day they burn the effigy of a character embodying the carnival. There are masked balls and processions of floats in the streets of the city as well as in Sitges (see p.66). (You can buy fancy dress at **Menkes,** see p. 91, and feathers at **La Plumista,** see p. 87.)

## MARCH

March 19 is San Josep's (St Joseph's) Day, patron saint of fathers and carpenters, and a very popular Christian name throughout Catalonia. It's celebrated by eating *crema catalana* (see p. 11, buy the necessary cooking utensils at **Caixa de Fang** see p. 97). Palm Sunday opens Holy Week and on Rambla de Catalunya, you can buy palm leaves woven into crosses, flowers, fantastic birds and so on. In the Mediterranean region, the palm tree is a symbol of regeneration and immortality On Easter Sunday godfathers give their godchildren a *mona*, a cake in the shape of a crown with several whole eggs set in it. The Easter egg represents life and perfection (buy them at **La Colmena** see p. 111).

## APRIL

Along with England, Catalonia celebrates Sant Jordi's (Saint George's) Day on 23 April. The patron saint had his hour of glory in the Middle Ages, when he slayed a dragon. The Catalan nobility adopted him as their emblem when they recaptured Catalonia from the Moors. On this day, a lover gives his sweetheart a rose and she in return gives him a book (**Sant Jordi** book-shop, see p. 109).

## MAY

On 11 May, the fair of Sant Ponç, patron saint of homeopaths, is a chance to buy medicinal and aromatic herbs. On Carrer de l'Hospital, stalls and stands sell delicious syrups, candied fruit and honey to the delight of the sweet-toothed. Barcelona still has around forty herbalist's shops with fragrant window displays dotted about the different areas of the city (see **Herboristeria Anormis** p.37).

## JUNE

In June, *Corpus Christi* celebrates the Eucharist. Since 1264, Christianity has taken over ancient processions designed to ripen the corn, and *caps grossos* ('big heads' and giants) parade through the streets. In Barcelona, the tradition of the *ou com balla* (dancing egg) has taken place in the cathedral cloisters and patio of the Casa del Ardiaca since the 18th century. An empty egg is balanced on the jet of the fountain. For some people this symbolic association of water and birth has a profound

religious significance. St John's Eve is 23 June, when the summer solstice is celebrated with bonfires. In the past, people used to burn old objects and furniture at crossroads, as a sign of

purification. Nowadays this is no longer allowed, except on Montjuïc Hill. Passing three times over the flames protects you from evil and people share *coca*, pine-kernel cake sprinkled with *barreja*, a mixture of malmsey, muscatel and spirits.

## JULY AND AUGUST

During the summer months, the famous *castells* are erected, and every Catalan dreams of becoming a *casteller* of his town. The 'castell' is the symbol of the community. For the townspeople, it means building a living castle by balancing one on top of another. Several volunteers form a muscular base onto which the rest climb. Groups compete to reach from five to nine levels. It's always a child, the *anxaneta*, who sets out to conquer the castle and waves to the crowd when he reaches the top. This Mediterranean tradition originated in ceremonies

designed to celebrate the earth's fertility. On 15 August the festival of Gràcia starts and for around two weeks there's drinking and dancing in the streets of the former village, which is now part of Barcelona. The people of Barcelona are extremely proud of their local traditions.

## SEPTEMBER

Catalonia's National Day (*Diada*) falls on 11 September and commemorates the taking of Barcelona by Felipe V in 1714. Local institutions were then abolished and the day has become the symbol of nationalism. It's not the defeat of the city that's being celebrated, but the fight against the Bourbons. There's a good deal of Catalan Flag waving on the *Diada*. On 24 September, the *Festes de la Mercè* are dedicated to the

Virgin Mary, who was made the patron saint of Barcelona in the 19th century. Since then, she's headed the bill at the *Festa Major*, when the city's inhabitants are in a kind of ferment, both secular and religious. Delicious local produce is on offer on every street corner, while giants and dragons drive out evil spirits. During the week of 24 September people attend musical and theatrical performances in the Sant Jaume, Cathedral and del Rei squares, Plaça Reial and Escorxador Park.

## NOVEMBER

All Saints' Day puts an end to the autumn festivities and celebration of abundance. Now it's time to remember the dead and turn fearsome beings into benevolent ancestors. In former times, on the eve of All Saints' Day, families would gather together to say rosaries for the dead while eating sweet chestnuts. The thick consistency of the chestnuts was supposed to block the way to roaming spirits, which people feared would try to take over the bodies of the living. Nowadays, you merely eat *panellets*, marzipan sweets covered in pine nuts in memory of the chestnuts, accompanied by a sweet wine.

## THE CATALONIAN LOCAL DANCE, THE *SARDANA*

The *sardana*, the quintessential Catalan dance, has very ancient, probably Cretan, origins. All generations take part in it and, after a brief introductory step, short eight-bar steps alternate with long sixteen-bar ones, repeated twice over. At the end, the dancers join hands in the centre of the circle. The band, or *cobla*, consists of eleven musicians playing the *flabiol* (a recorder played with one hand), the tambourine, two cornets, a *fiscorn*, two *tibles* (wind instruments) and the *tenora* (oboe), the instrument that symbolises the *sardana*. You can join in the dancing on Sundays at noon in the cathedral square and at 6.30pm in Sant Jaume Square (and you can buy your espadrilles for dancing at **Manual Alpargatera**, see p. 85).

# A FOOTBALL CRAZY CITY

With the unifying slogan 'More than a club', the legendary football team Barça has the loyalty of more than 108,000 members. From north to south its fans vow their unconditional support. When Barça wins, flags fly, horns sound and there's singing in the streets. And if you casually mention the magic word Barça when talking to a Catalan, you'll score an immediate hit and any wariness will vanish in a flash.

## THE BARÇA FOOTBALL CLUB

The club was founded in 1899, when Barcelona was beginning to aspire to be an important capital. The Great Exhibition of 1888 had launched it on its way and it was trying to become part of the European movement. Over a century has passed since the Swiss, Hans Gamper, founded this local institution. It's amusing to think that Barça, a symbol of the Catalan spirit, wears the red and blue of a Swiss province, and that the majority of the founder members were English or German.

## A SPIRIT OF INDEPENDENCE

Barça's matches against Real Madrid under Franco were a focus for the hatred of centralism. Its financial strength – it's the richest club in Europe, with an annual budget of 5.2 billion pesetas – and political attitude under the dictatorship constantly attracted enmity. Nowadays it remains the bastion of the Catalan spirit, combined with a desire to cross the Pyrenees in search of international recognition.

## BARÇA MUSEUM

Avinguda Aristides Maillol
☎ 93 496 36 00
Mon.-Fri. 10am-6pm,
Sat.-Sun. 10am-2pm
Entry charge.

The Barcelona Football Club Museum enjoys world fame for a museum of its kind and is the second most visited museum in the city. Photos, trophies, records and replays of match highlights portray the club's rich history. A biennial F.C. Barcelona art event brings together painters, sculptors and writers whose work is inspired by the sport. Thus artists such as Dalí, Clavé, Miró and Subirachs have added to the institution's prestige.

## FROM NORTH TO SOUTH

Gamper's stroke of genius was to name the club after the city. Barcelona Club has been instrumental in the integration of 'immigrants' from other parts of Spain. To be a *socio* (member) is in a way to become Catalan, by affiliation to a winning side. From the start, the founders regarded the institution as a place of union and true fraternity. It brings together people from every walk of life and membership cards are handed down from father to son.

## NOU CAMP

Inaugurated in September 1957, Nou Camp replaced the original and legendary Corts Stadium. A single stone from Corts Stadium became the foundation stone of the new stadium, thus ensuring

continuity. Designed by three architects, Soteras, Mitjans and Barbòn, it can hold 120,000 spectators and is the second largest stadium in the world.

## THE FOUNTAIN OF CANALETES

There's a place in Barcelona at the top of the Ramblas where people

gather to talk about sport. The Fountain of Canaletes, on the site of an ancient spring, was once the meeting-

place of strangers passing through the city. Nowadays it's where the latest match against Real Madrid is discussed and football takes on the air of a medieval joust. If you read a little Castilian Spanish buy a local daily, *la Vanguardia* or *el Periodico*, and, to complete the picture, dip into the famous novel by Manuel Vázquez Montalbán, *'Offside'* (published by Bourgois). At this rate, you'll soon be one of the four million Catalans not to go to bed on Sunday without first having found out the Barça results!

# ANTIQUES AND OLD LACE

Barcelona has a good choice of antiques shops and markets, so those who enjoy strolling around its narrow streets and ancient squares stand a chance of finding something interesting.

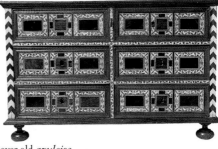

A diligent search can uncover old *azulejos*, ceramics, cooking utensils, a betrothal chest, *(caixa de nùvia)* or even an old edition of Tintin in Catalan. The flea market, Els Encants, is a good source for finds. It has a colourful sea of stalls with a mixture of old clothes and bric-a-brac.

## CATALAN FURNITURE

From the Middle Ages onwards, Catalonia was linked to the rest of Europe by sea. Overland transport remained more difficult, and furniture from the rest of Spain seldom found its way into the region. It was as rare to own a Spanish cabinet in Cordovan morocco, a *bargueno*, as it was a Chinese vase. Instead, furniture and other goods were imported from other countries such as England and France.

## AN AIR OF PROVENCE

In times gone by, carpenters from Provence settled in Girona and passed on secrets of their trade. You'll come across a great deal of this *masia* (farmhouse) furniture made of walnut, sometimes inlaid with light boxwood. Often, for reasons of economy, the front of the furniture was elaborately worked, while the back was left rough. Over the centuries carpenters worked in oak, walnut, silver birch, poplar and even mahogany imported from overseas.

## THE *CAIXA DE NUVIA*

The betrothal chest was an institution in Catalan families from the 16th to the 18th century. Generally made of walnut, it was around 140cm/55in long and 60cm/24in high and was used

for storage. It spread from the plains to the mountains and became common in both farmhouses and palaces. On their wedding day, the betrothed couple were each given a chest containing their dowry. The woman's had a small door, which opened to reveal a jewel compartment. In the 18th century, this traditional chest gave way to a chest of drawers, then a mirrored wardrobe, less mobile, but more practical for storing belongings.

At 8 Paja, they sell a fine selection of walking sticks with ivory, mother-of-pearl and silver knobs, as well as gorgeous ostrich-feather fans and vases made of glass similar in style to that of Gallé. At 11 Paja, Erika Niedermaier sells delicate 17th-century ceramics with metallic detail, apothecaries' ointment pots and a wide variety of wrought-iron objects, whose history this devoted collector will be only too pleased to tell you. At 17 Banys Nous, José Royo specialises in sacred art, gilded wood, popular sculpture, and interesting and unusual Baroque liturgical objects. At 14 Banys Nous, there are items of early Catalan furniture, betrothal chests and lovely old *azulejos* (a word derived from the Persian *'al zuleich'*, meaning a smooth flat stone), colourful enamelled tiles typical of the Iberian Peninsula (for opening times see p. 101).

## FROM ANTIQUES TO AZULEJOS

Antique lovers should make their way to the Call, the old ghetto of medieval Barcelona (see p. 37). Banys Nous and Paja streets are lined with antique shops.

(see p. 37)

(for opening times see p. 101).

---

### *L'ARCA DE L'AVIA,* THE STUFF OF DREAMS

**Banys Nous, 20**
☎ **93 302 15 98**
**Mon.-Fri.**
**10.30am-2pm, 5-8pm.**

Founded in 1840, these famous suppliers to the Spanish royal family made bobbin lace and Spanish *mantillas*. At that time, such frothy accessories were highly prized and, as with jewellery, the amount a woman wore was a sign of her wealth. This shop is a treasure chest (*arca*) of everything that once made up a bride's trousseau – embroidered linen tablecloths and sheets, damask bath towels and even the ceremonial cloth in which the dowry was sometimes placed.

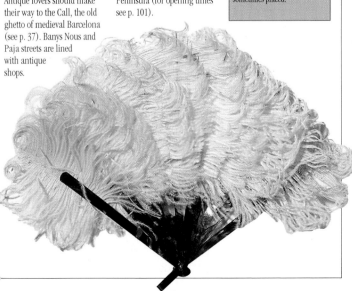

# MODERNISME – EXUBERANCE AND EXTRAVAGANCE ABOVE ALL

Barcelona is renowned for its superb *Modernista* architecture. From the Palau de la Música and hospital of San Pau to the Quatre Gats bar and Bolòs pharmacy, this artistic movement shaped houses like sculptures, covered façades with azure and gold, and added floral designs to chimneys. Everything defies logic and order, and imagination rules supreme.

On every street corner, you come face to face with the spirit of inventiveness and unusual detail that makes this city so fascinating.

## A FAMILY LIKENESS

Modernisme refers to a cultural movement that emerged at the end of the 19th century. It had similarities with the British Modern Style, Belgian 1900 Style, German Jugendstil, Viennese and Prague Sezessionstil, Italian Liberty and French Art Nouveau. It became famous because of its appropriation of the powerful *Renaixença* (1878), or the movement for a return to the Catalan identity. Writers, musicians and poets added their efforts to those of painters and architects to turn Modernisme into a lifestyle.

## AT THE TURN OF THE CENTURY

In the 19th century, people believed that progress and science would be the saviours of humanity. However, at the turn of the century, this thinking underwent a serious crisis, triggering anarchy and assassination attempts, and Barcelona was nick-named 'The Rose of Fire'. Subjectivity, irrationality, the return to nature, and oriental doctrines overtook order and reason. Modernisme was a reaction to academicism and provincial bad taste. Sustained by the profits of industrialisation and commerce, Modernisme found patrons in the wealthy inhabitants of Barcelona.

## THE ROOTS OF CATALAN ART

The desire to return to its origins was rooted in the desire to review the glories of the Catalonia's past and her achievements. In England, at the same time as this, the Pre-Raphelite Brotherhood (1848), the Arts and Crafts Movement (1888) and Symbolism were promoting spiritual art with a social purpose. The designer William Morris (1864-1896) relaunched the craft industry taking inspiration from nature, while in France Viollet-le-Duc (1814-1879) became fascinated by medieval bulidings.

## HOW TO RECOGNISE THE *MODERNISTA* STYLE

In the 19th century, eclectic architecture dominated the scene and buildings were a mixture of styles. They could display Egyptian, Roman, Moorish and Greco-Roman influences, as the university, (see p. 50), while the neo-Gothic style was also an unqualified success. *Modernista* architects distinguished themselves by the use they made of these sources of inspiration. Sinuous lines, asymmetry, dynamism, richness of detail and refinement were all of great importance.

## FROM STREET LIGHTS TO SHOP SIGNS

Modernisme regarded a design as a 'total work' integrating all the arts. It could be the result of collaboration between cabinetmakers, craftsmen in mosaics, ceramicists, jewellers, craftsmen in wrought iron, sculptors and master glass makers, all driven by attention to detail. From door handles to mosaic cladding, everything was carefully designed. Take a look at the hallways of *Modernista* buildings to appreciate the wealth of decorative detail used.

## KEEPING THE LADIES HAPPY

Barcelona still has some two hundred shops and clothing stores from this era, which were designed with women very much in mind. You can picture elegant ladies, dressed in velvet or damask choosing fabric for a new outfit, or selecting from the very latest,

## IN PURSUIT OF *MODERNISTA*

Wake up and have breakfast at the **Hotel Espana**. Go for a walk and shop for delicious chocolates at **Figueras**, rare stamps from philatelist **Monge** (see p. 102), and made-to-measure shirts at **Xanco** (see p. 46). Have a leisurely lunch on the terrace of **Asador de Aranda** or in the more formal setting of **Dama**. In the afternoon, visit the **Museu Nacional d'Art Modern de Catalunya** (see p. 53) and stop for refreshment at **Hivernacle**, pop into the **Macaya Palace** for a temporary exhibition, and in the evening go to a concert at the **Palau de la Música** (see p. 38), or to **Molino** to mix with the hoi polloi.

fashionable accessories. Some women would tie their ankles together in order not to tear the delicate fabric of their tight skirts, so it would appear that being a fashion victim is by no means a new thing…

# TOTAL DESIGN

'Make Barcelona beautiful', the slogan of the nineties, triggered an avalanche of innovative projects. Barcelona wanted to improve its appearance, and exploring it on foot, you'll discover open-air sculptures, smart traffic signs and state-of-the-art phone booths that amount to a kind of street art. From comic strips to coathangers, nothing escapes this creative fever, and modernity and the Catalan identity combine to stunning effect.

## AN ANCESTRAL TRADITION

Catalonia is at the cutting edge of Spanish design, but why here more than elsewhere? When the New World was discovered Catalans were harassed out of any form of trade with the Americas whatsoever. They never profited from the crock of gold which the Americas became and so devoted all their efforts to developing their own strengths

and resources. The result of this inward concentration of effort was a strong tradition of family cottage industries which have lasted throughout the centuries.

## IDEAS, BUT NO RAW MATERIALS

Like all countries lacking in raw materials (Japan, Sweden, Switzerland, etc.), Catalonia specialised in light manufacturing – textiles, glass, ceramics, leather, metallurgy, wood, paper and the graphic arts. *Modernisme* (see p.22) advocated the idea of the 'total work', arguing that an architect

ought to be able to produce the whole design, both outside and inside. This concept of symbiosis between raw materials and interior design was revived in the fifties by the generation of architects that included Oriol Bohigas, Josep Antoni Coderch and designers such as André Ricard and Oscar Tusquets.

## THE DESIGNERS – JACKS-OF-ALL TRADES

It isn't easy to classify the artists who move from one discipline to another – from architecture

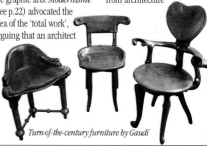

*Turn-of-the-century furniture by Gaudí*

to interior design, by way of fashion, ceramics and even graphics. Most representative of them all is perhaps Xavier Mariscal, the prodigious young designer of ceramics, posters, comic strips, wardrobes, shoes, and carpets. His mascot for the Olympic Games, 'Cobi', has become an international star just as its creator.

## DESIGN ORGANISATIONS

After forty years of Francoism the city has one more taken up its creative vocation. Today there are seven schools of design, and many design bodies. The oldest and most prestigious organisation is the FAD (Foundation of the Decorative Arts), which awards an annual prize to the best designer. Caixa, one of the biggest Spanish banks, is an outstanding contributor, providing ever-present support for science and the arts, continuing a very Catalan turn-of-the-century tradition of patronage (see the Güells, p. 29). In addition to this,

every two years in April, the city organises a 'Design Spring', a tour of galleries, shops and bars to make sur its inhabitants are ready for all the latest trends when the good weather starts. For more information, call
☎ 93 218 28 22.

## CATALAN SPECIALITIES

If you want to get into Catalan design, there's pler of choice – formal furnitur or crazy lamps by Mariscal and Cortès, an armchair with a 'Mantis' wooden she by Pep Bonnet, Mariscal furnishing fabric by Mariet or his 'duplex' stool with colourful wavy feet. More sober and timeless is the TMC lamp (1961) by Milà exhibited at the MoMA, or the Lluscà pressure cooker. All these designs have the distinctive feature of playing with different styles and influences (especially Italian) to invent a brand new style of their own, involving a concern for detail, materials and humour, and producing enormously creative designs.

# MIRÓ, PICASSO AND TÀPIES

B arcelona is synonymous with the genius of three great artists, Miró, Picasso and Tàpies. Each in turn was inspired to produce images of the city in keeping with his own particular vision. Miro transformed the world into a riot of colours and shapes, Picasso sketched locals and peasants with just a few strokes, while Tàpies experimented with collage and engraving techniques.

## JOAN MIRÓ

Born in 1893 in a small street in the heart of the Ciutat Vella (Old Town), Miró always remained very attached to Catalonia. He became an artist of international renown, but never forgot his homeland. His first exhibition was held in 1918 after which he divided his time between Spain and France. The Fondació Joan Miró (p.64) is a good way to see his work. Look for sculptures, lithographs, etchings, tapestries, ceramics, theatre sets and masks. The city is littered with monuments bearing his signature. To complete your whirlwind study you can also see exhibits of his work at the **Ceramica Museum** and then try a cocktail at **Boadas**, a bar (see p.64) which he frequented regularly.

## PABLO PICASSO

Born in Malaga, Picasso was barely fourteen years old when he arrived in Barcelona in 1895. He lived here for seven years before settling in Paris in 1904. His formative years were spent in a turn-of-

*Les Demoiselles d'Avignon.*

the-century climate much influenced by Modernisme (see p. 22). His studies of the Barceloneta, the dissident fringes of the Barrio Chino and his first Blue Period works (see **Museu Picasso** p. 38), reflect the misery pervading the Barcelona of 1900. He lived with his parents in the Plaça de la Mercè and studied at the **Llotja** Art School (see p. 40). Later he took a flat at 36 Nou de la Rambla and frequented the variety cafés of the Barrio Chino or El

*The Carrer d'Avinyo*

Raval, the city's red light district. The title of his famous painting *Les Demoiselles d'Avignon* (1906) was inspired by a brothel in the Carrer d'Avinyo frequented by sailors from the neighbouring port.

## ANTONI TÀPIES

It's difficult to separate the life and work of this artist born in 1923. All his creativity was channelled towards the service of the political. He was influenced by the Dadaist and Surrealist movements and turned his art into a free-thinking, provocative game. He developed an abstract style

which looked deceptively simple, including the use of symbols as a kind of sign language, and every day objects. Tàpies produced his first major works in 1945. For a thorough appreciation

### QUATRE GATS CAFÉ
**C. Montsiò, 3**
☎ **93 302 41 40**
**Closed Sun. lunchtime.**

This café opened in 1897, on the ground floor of a neo-Gothic building designed by the *Modernista* architect Puig i Cadafalch. The name 'Quatre Gats' is probably a tribute to the Chat Noir (Black Cat), a Parisian cabaret that Pere Romeu, one of the founders of the Quatre Gats, knew from having worked there. From 1897 to 1903, the Quatre Gats saw gatherings of the artists and writers of the day. Picasso designed the menu and held his first exhibition here in 1900.

of this artist visit the **Fundacio Antoni Tàpies** (see p.49). Then visit **Ediciones T**, the art gallery which specialises in graphic works and books (see p. 105). It also makes a point of exhibiting young Catalan and foreign talent.

# GAUDÍ: UTOPIA WITH A HEART

Antoni Gaudí is an architect inseparable from our idea of Barcelona. Both visionary and iconoclast, he is the embodiment of this surprising and intoxicating city. Born in 1852, he was a fervent nationalist and misanthropist, and very devout. Towards the end of the century, with the cultural and political rebirth and a new economic prosperity, the enlightened middle classes were eager to adopt the new European trends and Gaudí profited particularly from the patronage of Eusebio Güell.

## PARC GÜELL

Between 1900 and 1914, Gaudí wanted to create a garden-city along the lines of an English park, as a counterpoint to the growing industrialisation of the cities. His sponsor, Eusebi Güell (see box) was preoccupied with utopian social reforms. The area was originally barren but

Gaudí refused to have the ground levelled and subjected his architecture to the demands of the landscape. Slanting supporting columns make the paths look more like tunnels.

## CHAMELEON-LIKE ARCHITECTURE

At times, confusion sets in and it's hard to tell where Gaudí's designs begin and where nature ends. His work merges, chameleon-like, with the very ground on which it was based. Gaudí drew inspiration from everything, but beneath an apparently haphazard exterior, his work is very strict, and the fantastic shapes were designed with the help of detailed models. The residential area was supposed to have been divided up into

sixty parcels of land for houses, but only two were ever built, one of which is now the Gaudí museum. The project was never completed because Güell was afraid that it would eat up his entire fortune. Today, the two houses at the entrance to the park look like gingerbread houses or strange palaces built from odds and ends – hallucinogenic mushrooms with Moorish outlines and bold mosaics.

## SUCCESSFUL INTEGRATION

Further into the park a multicoloured salamander stands guard, whilst at the top a square edged by a long winding bench, with backrests in the shape of the human

form overlooks the city. Josep Maria Jujol, Gaudí's assistant, collaborated with him on the project. They used broken ceramics as decoration reviving the Arab tradition of *azulejos* and thus preceding the Dadaist and Cubist collages. Whatever your artistic preferences, a walk through this amazing park

is a must. There is nothing like it anywhere else in the world (Carretera Carmel ☎ 93 284 64 46. Every day 10am-6pm in winter, 9am-8pm in summer).

## LA SAGRADA FAMÍLIA

The first stone of this church dedicated to the Holy Family was laid in 1883. Liké the Sacré-Coeur in Paris, it was built with the help of donations from the public. Its design and building occupied Gaudí for forty years. However, sadly only the east façade depicting the life of Christ was finished before Gaudí's untimely death in 1926, when he was killed by a tram. Unfortunately in 1936 all Gaudí's plans were destroyed by the Anarchists and so his designs could never be carried through to completion. However, work began once more towards the end of the 1950s, causing great contoversy, and continues to this day under the watchful eye of Jordi Bonet. This building is an exuberant flight of fantasy. Eight towers twist upwards into the sky, an extravaganza in stone which everyone can appreciate for its boldness and uniqueness, no matter what their individual tastes and preferences may be. Another 'must' on your visit to the city. (Plaça de la Sagrada Família ☎ 93 455 02 47. Every day 9am-6pm in winter, 9am-8pm in summer. Entry charge.)

## THE GÜELL FAMILY

Juan Antonio Güell used to boast that all the 'good families' of turn-of-the-century Barcelona came to his house in Pedralbes – aristocrats, the wealthy upper middle-classes, the 'nouveaux riches' and *indianos* with legendary fortunes. The latter group, to which the Güell family belonged, symbolised success, social climbing and prestige in the Spanish colonies. On their return to the city, they started a textile business and built palaces and parks. Eusebi Güell, the son of the founder of the line, became Antoni Gaudí's patron and commissioned many projects from him.

# What to see Practicalities

On one side you have the Sierra de Colserola and, on the other, the blue Mediterranean — two unmistakable landmarks that make it easy to find your way in Barcelona. When Catalans give an address, they always also say whether the street number faces the mountains or the sea. Traffic flows freely in the Eixample, where the avenues are dead straight. Only the old quarters are narrower, but the steeples of the cathedral, Santa Maria del Mar, and of the del Pi church will help you get your bearings. Don't be afraid to explore the labyrinth of medieval alleyways in the old town — you won't get lost for long and it's the best way to really get to know the place. So go ahead — a fascinating city lies in wait for you!

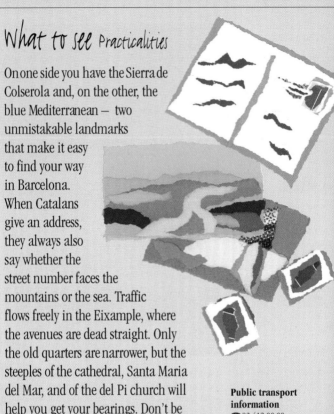

**Public transport information**
☎ 93 412 00 00

**Lost property**
☎ 93 402 31 61.

**Guardia Urbana**
This is a service reserved for tourists in the event of theft, accident or loss of documents: La Rambla, 43,
☎ 93 301 90 60.
Open in the winter from 7am to midnight and in the summer from 7am to 2pm.

## GETTING AROUND BARCELONA

Visit the old quarters (Raval, Ribera, and Gòtico) on foot and stroll around them at your leisure. The Eixample, criss-crossed by a network of wide avenues, is served by a number of bus routes and metro stations. The numerous taxis are among the cheapest in the European Union. You'll need them for going to the Güell Park and the Sagrada Familia, which are not in the city centre.

## THE METRO

Air-conditioned and clean, it runs from Monday to Thursday from 5am to 11pm, on Friday and Saturday until 1am, and on Sunday from

## BY BIKE OR ROLLER BLADES

At weekends, Barcelona residents frequently hire bikes or roller blades to ride or skate along the waterfront or Diagonal. It's the ideal place for cycling enthusiasts and those who enjoy unusual walks. The place to go to hire a bike is opposite the Francià station: **Bicitram** Av. Marquès de Argentera, 15, ☎ 93 792 28 41. Open Sat., Sun. and public holidays. You can hire two-wheelers for 350 ptas an hour here. Bike hire is also available on the Diagonal near the Corte Inglès, and at the Vila Olimpica.

6am to midnight. In addition there are a few FGC (Ferro-carrils de la Generalitat de Catalunya) suburban city rail lines which link up with the metro, the most useful of which goes to the Tibidabo. Tickets costs 130 ptas, but for the duration of your stay it's worth buying a T1 ticket (700 ptas), which entitles you to 10 journeys by bus and metro. You're restricted to travelling on the metro with the T2 ticket. In addition, there are 1-day (500 ptas), 3-day (1,200 ptas) and 5-day (1,800 ptas) travel passes for bus and metro.

The 3 and 5-day passes can be bought in the commercial department of the Universitat station, Monday to Friday 8am to 8pm. Important intersections on these lines are Passeig de Gràcia, Catalunya, and Diagonal.

## BUSES

Numerous bus lines cover the whole city. Buses operate from 6.30am to 10pm, and some continue right through to 4am. (Nitbus). You can tell which are which by their numbers and can consult the maps on bus shelters that give details of their routes. The Tomb bus is the most useful; it goes from Catalunya square to Pius XII square. Although more expensive, it runs every 5 to 10 minutes. Finally, there's a Tibibus that takes you from Catalunya square to Tibidabo square Saturday and Sunday throughout the year, and every day in July and August, from 10.30am to 8.30pm; it's ideal for visiting the Tibidabo amusement park.

## BY CAR

If you rent a car for the week-end, be very careful about where you park it. It will cost you 15,000 ptas to free it from the city car pound. When you do find a space, which is not easy, don't leave any valuables in sight as thefts are frequent. Daytime car parks are reasonably safe (around 250 ptas per hour, 3,000 ptas a day).

**Avis,** Arago, 235,
☎ 93 487 87 54,
🄵 93 487 20 50 or
☎ 93 478 17 06 (at airport).

**Europcar,** Consell de Cent, 363,
☎ 93 488 23 98
🄵 93 488 21 92.

**Hertz,** Tuset, 10,
☎ 93 217 32 48,
🄵 93 217 80 76.

## TAXIS

The city is swarming with 11,000 yellow and black taxis. The green light shows they're available. This mode of transport is still very reasonable and they rarely refuse to take you, even for very short distances.

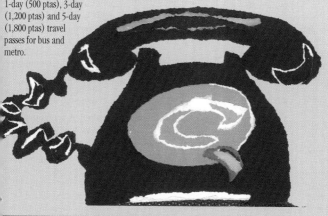

Over 1,000 taxis even accept credit cards. Allow 270 ptas for picking up, then 100 ptas per km/0.5mile. A supplement is charged for luggage, airport transfers and animals .

**Barnataxi**
☎ 93 357 77 55.

**Taxi Radio Movil**
☎ 93 358 11 11.

**Radio Taxi**
☎ 93 225 00 00.

### BY TRAIN

To get to Sitges (see p. 66), just take a train from Passeig de Gràcia station (RENFE station) or Sants station. Air-conditioned trains operate every 15 minutes from 6am to 11pm. and the journey to this charming seaside resort takes 35 minutes. Don't forget to date stamp your ticket, otherwise you risk getting fined!

### MAKING A PHONE CALL

The international country code for Spain is 34. The code for Barcelona is 93. When dialling a local number from within Barcelona you must

also ensure that you dial this 93 at the beginning - the codes were changed in 1998, making the old seven digit numbers nine digits. All the numbers in Spain now have nine digits and you dial all nine from wherever you are calling.

Public telephone booths have a distinctive modern design and are blue and green in colour. Calls are very expensive, and you'll never have enough coins to make an international call. It's much better to buy a phone card (for 1,000 or 2,000 ptas), at a tobacconist's. Failing this, try the **locutorios telefonicos**, pay-phones installed at Rambla, 88, ☎ 93 412 70 26, ❶ 93 412 72 39, open every day 10am-11pm, and at Sants station, Mon.-Sat. 8am-10.30pm, Sun. 9am-10.30pm.

### WRITING HOME
**Oficina Central**
Pl. Antoni Lopez, 1,
☎ 93 318 38 31.
Metro Barceloneta or Jaume I.

The impressive main post office is situated at the lower end of the Via Laietana. It's open Monday to Friday from 8am to 10pm, Saturday from 8am to 8pm and Sunday from 9am to 2pm. To send a postcard within Europe it will cost you 30 ptas, for a postcard or letter weighing up to 20gm, it will cost 115 ptas to USA and Canada and 185 ptas to Australasia. You can buy stamps from *estanques* or a tobacconist's. Letterboxes (mailboxes) are easy to spot – they're large with yellow lettering and are found at crossroads.

### BUREAUX DE CHANGE

Banks are open Mon. to Fri. from 8.30am to 2pm, Sat. from 8.30am to 1pm (closed in summer).

**American Express :**
Passeig de Gràcia, 101,
☎ 93 217 00 70.

Open Mon. to Fri. from 9.30am to 6pm and Sat. from 10am to noon. Foreign currency can be changed every day at the airport at Banco Exterior de

España from 7.30am to 10.45pm, and every day at Sants station from 8am to 10pm (except 1 and 6 January; and 25 and 26 December). The same applies in the city centre, at the offices of

### Exact Change

Av. Catedral, 1 or La Rambla, 130. Open every day from 9am to 10pm .

### Cheque Point

La Rambla, 64. Open every day from 9am to midnight.

## TOURIST INFORMATION OFFICES

### Turismo de Barcelona

Tarragona, 149-157,
☎ 93 423 18 00,
🄵 93 423 26 49.

This is the address of the administrative centre, which isn't open to the public. It's nevertheless useful if you wish to obtain information in advance of your arrival.

Once you have arrived safely in Barcelona you can go to the following tourist information offices, where you'll be given maps and information on the city (ask especially for brochures on the subject of Miró, *Modernisme*, Gaudí, New Urbanism, and Quadrat d'Or).

### At the airport:

Aeropuerto del Prat, 08820 Barcelona

Terminal A: ☎ 93 325 58 29/
☎ 93 478 47 04

Terminal B: ☎ 93 478 05 65/
93 478 05 68

Open every day from 9.30am to 8pm, except for Sun. when it closes at 3pm.

### At Sants station:

Pl. de Països Catalans, s/n - L'Estació de Sants
08014 - Barcelona
☎ 93.491.44.31

Open Mon. to Fri. from 8am to 8pm, Sat., Sun. and public holidays from 8am to 2pm, during the summer, every day from 8am to 8pm.

### In the Eixample:

Gran Via de les Corts Catalanes, 658
☎ 93 301 74 43
🄵 93 412 25 70.

Open Mon. to Fri. from 9am to 7pm and Sat. 9am to 2pm.

### On the Ramblas:

Palau de la Virreina, La Rambla, 99,
☎ 93 301 77 75.

Open Mon. to Fri. 10am to 2pm. and 4pm to 8pm; during the summer, Mon. to Sat. 9.30am to 9pm, and Sun. 10am to 2pm.

In July and August, hostesses

wearing red and white uniforms and 'Turismo de Barcelona' badges are assigned to strategic points and will be able to provide you with information.

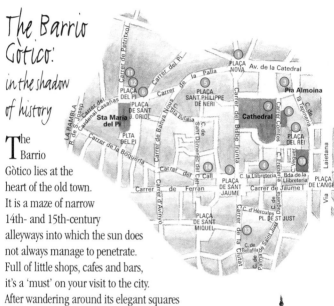

# The Barrio Gòtico:
## in the shadow of history

The Barrio Gòtico lies at the heart of the old town. It is a maze of narrow 14th- and 15th-century alleyways into which the sun does not always manage to penetrate. Full of little shops, cafes and bars, it's a 'must' on your visit to the city. After wandering around its elegant squares and museums take a little refreshment in the Plaça del Pi and try a *tortilla* washed down with *horchata* (barley drink).

### ❶ Plaça Nova★★

The ancient city of *Barcino*, whose name is carved in the square, was founded here. The remains of the 4th-century city walls contain two Roman towers flanking the del Bisbal Gate. One of them has a hollowed-out niche dedicated to St Roch, the patron saint, whose feast-day is celebrated in full summer on 16th August. There is also an antiques market on Thursdays, Advent celebrations, and *sardana* dancing on Sundays. The 18th-century Baroque façade of the bishop's palace adds cachet to the setting. The same can't be said of the College of Architects built in 1961, though it does have a frieze by Picasso.

### ❷ The Cathedral★★★
Mon.-Sun.
8am-1.30pm, 4-7.30pm
Terrace open Mon.-Sat. morn.
9.30am-12.30pm, 4-6.30pm
Museum ☎ 93 310 25 80
Every day 11am-1pm.
Entry charge.

The magnificent Gothic façade actually dates from the 19th century. The cathedral dedicated to St Eulàlia was founded in the 13th century and completed in the 15th. Its claim to fame is that it contains precious liturgical objects, such as the famous 16th-century *Christ of Lepanto* crucifix, said to have been on board the Spanish flagship of Don Juan of Austria at the time of the decisive victory against

the Turks in 1571. The baptismal fonts are said to have been used to christen the first six Indians brought back by Christopher Columbus in 1493. The delightful cloister is planted with orange-trees, magnolias, medlars and palm-trees. It's a cool oasis and a haven of peace that is sometimes broken by the cries of thirteen geese, their number symbolising Eulàlia's age at the time of her martyrdom.

### ❸ Pia Almoina and Diocesan Museum★★
Av. de la catedral, 4
☎ 93 315 22 13
Tue.-Sat. 10am-2pm, 5-8pm
Sun. 11am-2pm
Entry charge.

This medieval institution next to the cathedral was once an alms house providing a hundred poor people a day with a meal. Its subtle conversion to a Diocesan Museum is very successful, and is well worth climbing the few steps for.

### ❹ Catalonia Excursion Centre★★
Carrer del Paradis, 10
Tue.-Sat. 10am-2pm, 4-8pm,
Sun. 10am-2pm
Free entry.

You're treading on the remains of the Roman city here. A mill wheel embedded in the ground marks the entrance to the site. At the summit of *Mons Taber*, a temple dedicated to Augustus, built in the 1st century, was visible from far away. The columns you can see today were found at the start of the 20th century, while the bells of the nearby cathedral are a reminder that gods have been worshipped on this mound for thousands of years.

### ❺ Plaça de Sant Felip Neri and Shoe Museum★★
☎ 93 301 45 33
Every day 11am-2pm,
closed Mon.
Entry charge.

This shady little square often by-passed by visitors short of time occupies the site of a former cemetery. The Baroque façade of the church and two 16th-century houses form a harmonious group. The emblems of the Guilds of Shoemakers and Coppersmiths – the lion of St Mark and two spoons – are clearly visible. In the Shoe Museum, you can't miss the foot measuring 1.22m/4ft that was used as a model for the Christopher Columbus monument.

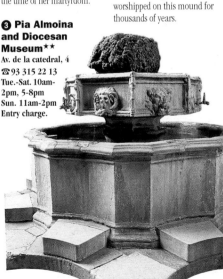

### ❻ Plaça del Pi and church★★★
**Every day 9am-1pm, 5-8.30pm. Free entry.**

The del Pi church is a perfect example of 14th-century Catalan Gothic. The square with one pine-tree (*pi*) is delightful. In summer, sit on the terrace, sipping iced coffee and lulled by the sound of a saxophone. In winter, during Advent, the façades sparkle with a thousand lights. A slightly Bohemian air gives the place its charm.

### ❼ Plaça de Sant Jaume ★★

The institutional centre of the city that was once the site of the forum, the public square in Roman times. The name *Jaume* (James) comes from the church that stood here until 1824. Today the Town Hall (*Ajuntament)* and Province of Catalonia (*Generalitat)* are in political opposition here. On feast days (Sant Jordi's and Sant Mercé's, see p.15), the *castells* — pyramids of acrobats balancing precariously on top of one

another — defy the laws of gravity, while the three flags of Spain, Barcelona and Catalonia flutter in the breeze.

### ❽ Museu Frederic Marés★★★
**Plaça St Iu, 5**
☎ **93 310 58 00**
**Tue.-Sat. 10am-5pm, Sun. 10am-2pm**
**Entry charge.**

In fine weather, pause on the patio, where tables and refreshments await you. The museum houses a survey of Spanish sculpture from the Middle Ages to the 19th century. If there are too many versions of *Virgin Mary with Child* and *Descent from the Cross*, for your liking, go

upstairs and see the collection of briar pipes, fob watches, pince-nez, parasols and fans.

### ❾ Plaça del Rei, Tinell and Chapel of St Agatha★★★
☎ **93 315 11 11**
**Jul. to Sep., Tue.-Sat. 10am-2pm, 4-8pm, Sun. 10am-2pm.**
**Entry charge.**

This is the most remarkable group of buildings in the city. Climb the palace steps to reach the Saló del Tinell, the magnificent hall and throne room, built in the 14th century. It is here in this very room that the Catholic King Ferdinand and Queen Isabella, on a visit to Barcelona, received Columbus on his

return from the New World in 1493. On the walls, 13th-century frescoes illustrate this period of Catalan grandeur. The 14th-century palace chapel of St Agatha is adorned with a renowned 15th-century painting, the *Constable's Altar-piece*, by Huguet. From the top of King Martí's turret you can see a maze of alleyways overlooked by a cluster of steeples.

## ⑩ Museu d'Historia de la Ciutat★★
**Combined entry ticket includes the Tinell.**

This museum dedicated to the history of the city is housed in the beautiful 15th-century mansion, Casa Clariana-Padellas. You can see extensive Roman ruins discovered during work carried out in the 1930s and the remains of a Christian basilica.

## ⑪ La Granja Dulcinea★
**Carrer Petritxol, 2
☎ 93 302 68 24
Mon.-Sun. 9am-1pm, 4-9pm.**

A *granja* is a bit like a tearoom, where fresh farm produce takes pride of place. Highly recommended is the *suisso con ensaimada*, thick hot chocolate topped with whipped cream and accompanied

by Majorcan cakes and pastries, all beneath the understanding eye of the old man in the photo pinned to the wall. Don't worry, everyone in Barcelona, young and old alike, indulge themselves here.

## ⑫ La Gavineteria Roca★★
**Plaça del Pi, 3
☎ 93 302 12 41
Mon.-Fri. 9.45am-1.30pm, 4.15-8pm, Sat. 10am-2pm, 5-8pm.**

Roca sells bladed instruments of all kinds. There's been a knife grinder here since 1911, specialising in cut-throat razors, manicure sets, scissors, knives and penknives. The *navaja de Albacete* with a curved handle will cost you 2,000 ptas. The extraordinary stainless-steel *Modernista* shop front, however, is not for sale.

## ⑬ Anormis★★
**Carrer de la Ciutat
☎ 93 302 30 04
Mon.-Fri. 8am-2pm, 4-8pm.**

Entering this, one of the oldest shops in the old town, you may well come across the very herb you've been seeking for ages. Señor Anormis acts as

## ⑭ THE *CALL*

The *Call* (alley) or ghetto conjures up one of the most flourishing facets of medieval Barcelona, the aljama, or Jewish community. Nowadays finding any trace of it would require special powers to see beyond the stones. The bloody pogrom of 1391 caused fire and bloodshed. Now nothing remains but memories of the ambassadors, interpreters, financiers, astronomers, alchemists and eminent doctors who used to live and work here. Only Carreres del Call, Sant Ramon del Call and Sant Domènec del Call bear witness to the past.

herbalist, doctor, confidant and adviser to his customers and his formulae are only revealed in the strictest secrecy.

# The Ribera:
## past meets present

Living in the Ribera is like living in a village. Old crafts rub shoulders with fashionable institutions. The shop window of a humble upholsterer vies with the fashionable Galeria Maeght. Surrounded by streets which are steeped in history, the church of Santa Maria del Mar stands on what was once the shore in the 14th-century. It suffered damage during the Civil War and is particularly loved by the local people.

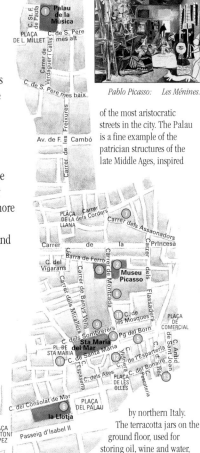

*Pablo Picasso:* Les Ménines.

of the most aristocratic streets in the city. The Palau is a fine example of the patrician structures of the late Middle Ages, inspired

## ❶ Palau de la Música★★★
Sant Francesc de Paula, 2
☎ 93 268 10 00
Jun-Jul., Sep.-Oct.
(closed Aug.)
Guided tour (charge)
Mon.-Fri. 2 and 3pm
Phone in advance
Concerts Sun. morning.

This palace was built in 1908 in the pure *Modernista* style by Domenech i Montaner. Specialists in the art of stained-glass windows, ceramics, mosaics and sculpture all collaborated in its construction. It has an elaborate façade supported on three large columns. The accoustics are excellent.

by northern Italy.
The terracotta jars on the ground floor, used for storing oil, wine and water, show that the original

## ❷ Museu Picasso★★★
Carrer Montcada, 15-19
☎ 93 319 63 10
Tue.-Sat. 10am-8pm,
Sun. 10am-3pm
Bookshop and restaurant
Entry charge.

Since 1963 the Palau Berenguer d'Aguilar has housed the works of Pablo Picasso. It opens onto one

inhabitants were involved in trade. On the first floor, some of Picasso's youthful works evoke his brief, but intense encounter with Barcelona's Bohemian set. The room devoted to his interpretation of Velàsquez's famous painting *Las Meninas* is the highlight of a visit to the museum.

### ❸ Museu du Tèxtil i d'Indumentària★★
Carrer Montcada, 12
☎ 93 310 45 16
Tue.-Sat. 10am-8pm,
Sun. 10am-3pm
Entry charge.

This museum is housed in the Palau de Los Marqueses De Llió, a Gothic masterpiece whose original structure has been preserved. You can sample some homemade pastries on the patio before seeing the collections. The Textile and Costume Museum traces the development of textiles over a period of 1,500 years, with precious Coptic cloth, Chantilly lace, embroidered damask, Indian calico, and creations by Worth and Balenciaga. Also on display are Catalan textile industry tools. Before leaving the palace, buy a few metres of fabric designed by Mariscal (3,300 ptas a metre/yard), the king of Barcelona design.

### ❹ Santa Maria del Mar★★★
Plaça Santa Maria
Every day
9am-1.30pm, 4.30-8pm.

Situated on the waterfront, the church was originally called *Santa Maria de las Arenas* (of the sands). This early 14th-century Gothic building symbolises the prosperity of the merchants of the period. Many sail makers, stevedores and porters are buried in its walls. Built

over half a century with remarkable unity of style, it has a wide nave and narrow aisles. In the Middle Ages Catalan sailors set sail for distant conquests to the cry of *Santa Maria*, their patron saint.

### ❺ Passeig del Born★★

The location for a market in medieval times, which sold goods from overseas including spices and medicines, it has a grisly past. Heretics condemned to death by the Spanish Inquisition were burned at the stake here. The Born was later turned into an open-air theatre and jousts (*bournar*), tournaments and other knightly celebrations took place. In 1874, the Merecat del Born was erected, a metal-structured market hall, nowadays used for temporary exhibitions.

### ❻ La Llotja★
**Pla del Palau, 22**
**Mon.-Fri. 10.30am-1pm.**

La Llotja was a typically Mediterranean institution and very powerful. Originally, this market hall was open to the elements, but in 1380 as business prospered and trade multiplied, a permanent building was erected. The *Consulat del Mar*, linked to the community of Catalan merchants overseas, was established here. Rebuilt in the 18th century, the low Gothic hall has been preserved and now houses the Stock Exchange and Academy of Fine Arts.

### ❼ Pla de la Garsa★
**Carrer Assaonadors, 13**
☎ 93 315 24 13
**Mon.-Sat. 1-4pm, 8pm-1am, Sun. 8pm-1am.**

A short distance from the Picasso Museum, this wine bar has the charm of an old-fashioned bistrot. A broken tiled floor surrounds the bar made of *rajoles* (terracotta tiles) from Valencia. The wrought-iron spiral staircase is the pride of the owner, who'll recommend the *embotits i formatjes*, an

excellent selection of cold ham and ewe's cheese washed down with a Rioja or Penedès wine (around 2,500 ptas).

*Wassili Kandinsky at the Galeria Maeght.*

### ❽ Galeria Maeght★
**Carrer Montcada, 25**
☎ 93 310 42 45
**Tue.-Sat. 10am-2pm, 4-8pm.**

*Aimé Maeght (1906-1981) opened this Barcelona temple to contemporary art in 1974. Housed in the 15th-century Cervelló palace, it exhibits works by Kandinsky, Braque, Miró and Tàpies, as well as less well-known artists such as Bennassar, Grau and Solano. You can purchase art books here, of course, but also graphic works by talented young artists and even collector's editions.*

### ❾ La Casa Gispert★★★
**Carrer Sombrerers, 23**
☎ 93 319 75 35
**Mon.-Fri. 8.30am-1.30pm, 3.30-7.30pm, Sat. 10am-1pm, 5-8pm.**

Since 1851 the Gispert family have been *Mestres Torradors*, past masters in the art of coffee-roasting. From the gleaming black-and-gold shop front wafts the sweetish smell of saffron, cinnamon and Ethiopian coffee. Sacks and jars overflow with dried fruits and spices as in an Oriental market. In the back shop, the old almond-grilling oven is still going strong. A charming place and a delightful way to indulge the senses.

### ⑩ L'Euskal Etxea★
**Placeta Montcada, 1-3**
☎ 93 310 21 85
**Tue.-Sun. morning
12.30-3pm,
7.30-11.30pm.**

For *tapas* fans this restaurant recommends a typical Basque selection – *txakas* (crab mayonnaise), *pimientos del piquillo* (green peppers) and mussel kebabs, accompanied by a local white *txacoli*, are all the rage. This is a charming typically *Euskera* (Basque) restaurant, which also houses a cultural centre.

### ⑪ Ici et Là★★
**Plaça Santa Maria del Mar, 2**
☎ 93 268 11 67
**Mon. lunchtime-Sat.
10.30am-2.30pm,
4.30-8.30pm.**

A simple yet sophisticated shop opening onto a square cooled by the spray from a Gothic fountain. Small pieces of iron furniture, multicoloured mosaic tables and ethnic objects mingle with the creations of young designers, which include brightly-coloured tablecloths with contrasting traditional Catalan designs (a pair of tea towels costs 1,550 ptas).

### ⑫ Vidrieria Grau★★
**Carrer Vidrieria, 6**
☎ 93 319 40 46
**Mon.-Fri. 9.30am-1.30pm,
4.30-8pm,
Sat. 9.30am-1.30pm.**

An astonishing array of time-worn shelves line the walls from floor to ceiling, with a display of glassware and opalines (starting at 3,000 ptas). See if you can unearth a treasure from among the dusty bric-a-brac. Founded in 1837, this shop has the old-fashioned charm of yesteryear. Olga Xirinacs talks with feeling about her family, who have been glass artists for twelve generations.

### ⑬ REC CONTAL

The tanning and dyeing industries were set up on the banks of the stream that gave this street its name. The street names of the Ribera evoke the ancient crafts which were practised in them: *Assaonadors, Blanqueria, Corretger, Vidrieria, Corders, Carders, Argenteria, Flassaders* and *Esparteria* (tanning, tawing, welding, stained-glass window making, rope-making, carding, silversmithing, blanket-making and working with rushes). The shop-keeping mentality was born here and the Catalans have a nose for business.

# The Raval:
## venture outside the old city walls

Better known as the Barrio Chino, the Raval has fascinated artists for a long time, with its pimps and prostitutes, transvestites, shady deals and more than a whiff of sleaze from the nearby port. For some years now though, cultural institutions have been moving in, adding a little respectability to the area. It is a cosmopolitan mix of locals and immigrants from Africa and India.

### ❶ Casa de la Caritat★★
**Carrer de Montalegre, 5-7**
☎ 93 412 07 81
Tue., Thu, Fri. 11am-2pm, 4-8pm, Wed. and Sat. 11am-8pm, Sun. 11am-7pm
Entry charge.

A perfect example of the new in the midst of the old. Built in 1714 on the site of a 14th-century convent, it used to be an asylum and workhouse, but is now used for exhibitions of town planning, being the home of the Centre de Cultura Contemporania. The superb patio (1714) and the façade (1993) again mix the old with the new. At the back there is a lovely little café with a terrace.

### ❷ Museu d'Arte Contemporani★★★
**Plaça dels Angels, 1**
☎ 93 412 08 10
Summer Mon.-Sat. 10.30am-8pm, Thu. 10pm, Sun. 11am-7pm, cl. Tue. Winter Mon., Wed., Fri. noon-8pm, Thu. 9.30pm, Sat. 10am-8pm, Sun. 10am-3pm. Entry charge.

The building was designed by the architect Richard

Meier, very much a fan of whiteness and purity. This dazzling liner of a building is in absolute contrast to the nearby façades of the old buildings around it. Opened in 1995 it displays a good

selection of work by mainly Catalan and Spanish artists since 1945, though there is some foreign work too. Also known as MACBA for short.

## ❸ Hospital de la Santa Creu★★
**Carrer del Carme, 47-49/c de l'Hospital, 56**
**Patio every day 10am-6pm.**

Take a walk in the shade of the former 15th-century hospital garden, once a refuge for pilgrims in Catalonia. The vestibule of the Casa de Convalescencia is sumptuously decorated with ceramic scenes of the life of St Paul in green and yellow. Gaudí died here in 1926.

## ❹ Sant Pau del Camp Monastery★★
**Carrer de Sant Pau, 101**
**☎ 93 441 00 01**
**Tue.-Sat. 7.30-8.45pm, Sun. 9.30am-1.30pm.**

To escape the hustle and bustle of the street, step inside Sant Pau, the 12th-century Romanesque Benedictine monastery where you'll be struck by the tranquillity of the cloister. The parish priest will gladly give you an account of its history, if asked.

## ❺ Palau Güell★
**Carrer Nou de la Rambla, 3-5**
**☎ 93 317 39 74**
**Mon.-Sat. 10am-2pm, 4-8pm**
**Entry charge.**

This enigmatic palace was built in 1888 by Gaudí for his patrons, the Güell family. A tour of the building takes you through a turn-of-the-century interior with

### BARRIO CHINO

The Barrio Chino, or Chinatown, owes its name to a report by the writer Francis Carcoi entitled 'China Town', yet you won't find a trace of Chinese immigration here. The district has been inhabited by Andalusians since the beginning of the 19th century. Pakistanis and Africans arrived recently to join them, making the Barrio Chino a kind of Catalan melting-pot.

Gaudí's curved and twisting shapes, whilst the façade displays his supreme artistry in wrought-iron work. The architect's fervent nationalism is apparent in the form of an eagle holding the coat of arms of Catalonia.

## ❻ El Indio★
**Carrer Carmen, 24**
**☎ 93 317 54 42**
**Mon.-Sat.**
**10am-2pm, 4.30-8pm.**

This is certainly one of the most attractive *Modernista* shop fronts in the city, but do go in and have a look around. The décor hasn't changed much for years with colourful remnants of cloth displayed on wooden racks and a cashier patient behind the till.

## ❼ Bar Muy Buenas★★
**Carrer Carme, 63**
**☎ 93 241 60 86**
**Tue.-Sat. 8am-9pm.**

One of the best-preserved *Modernista* bars. Order a *tallat* (coffee diluted with milk) or have your *bocata* (elevenses) with Serrano ham. A tempting array of drinks and snacks awaits you.

*The interior of Palau Güell.*

# The Ramblas: a place to see and be seen

La Rambla is at the heart of the city. The most famous street in Barcelona is lined with cafes, bars, shops, hotels and newspaper kiosks. It is always busy, no matter what time of day you arrive, though evening is undoubtedly when there is the most activity. In the morning little old ladies clutching string bags trot from the market to the Betlem church. In the evening three-card tricks, paintings and improvised acrobatics extract money from passers-by. The street cuts through the old town and the area which is known as the Ramblas.

## ❶ Plaça de Catalunya★

This large and irregularly-shaped square is the link between the old town and 19th-century Eixample, and was first landscaped in 1854. It became the nerve centre of the city in 1925 with the building of the department store, El Corte Inglès, banks and hotels. Marks & Spencer now has a store here. On Sundays, you can buy *pipas* (sunflower seeds) to feed to the pigeons.

## ❷ Església de Betlem★★★

**Rambla 107**
**Every day 7.45am-9pm.**
The façade is a Baroque flight of fancy, with statues of St Ignacio de Loyola and St Francisco de Borja deep in conversation. Begun in 1681, the church formed the nucleus of a complex of buildings occupied by the Jesuits until their expulsion in 1767. Sadly, the interior was gutted by fire during the Civil War in 1936. In the morning the low angle of the sun casts a theatrical light on one of the city's unique Baroque monuments.

### ❸ Palau de la Virreina★★★
Rambla 99
☎ 93 301 77 75.
Tue.-Sat. 11am-9pm,
Sun. 11am-3pm.
Entry charge.

The name comes from the Vice-reine of Peru, who occupied it after the death of her husband. A graceful 18th-century addition to the district, it then became the site for exhibitions of the decorative arts. Take the main staircase and see the superb French-style decor.

### ❹ La Boquería Market★★★
Ramblas 85-89. Every day except Sun. 6am-9.30pm.

Stroll round this covered market dating from 1860 and and enjoy the wonderful mediterranean feel. The locals chatter as they go round selecting the day's best buy and the stall holders call out to customers. The displays of fresh produce really are something to behold. If you wish to really blend in with the locals, stand at the *barra*, the bar, of the *Pinocho* kiosk and sample Catalan-style tripe.

### ❺ Liceu★
Ramblas, 61-65.

The opera house, a symbol of 19th-century middle-class and industrial Barcelona, was built in 1844 and burnt down for the first time in 1861. It was rebuilt, and came to be regarded as the finest opera house in Spain. However in 1893 it suffered a bomb attack and was damaged one more. It went up in flames again in 1994, but has just been restored. Fingers crossed this time.

### ❻ Hotel Oriente★
Rambla, 45,
☎ 93 302 25 58.

Built on the site of the Franciscan College of St Bonaventura, of which only the old cloister was preserved. In its heyday, people such as Hemingway stayed here, as well as various Hollywood stars and toreadors. In the 19th century it was still one of the biggest hotels in Europe and in 1975 Antonioni filmed *The Passenger* here with Jack Nicholson.

### ❼ Plaça Reial★★
Under the 19th-century arcades it's a fascinating mix of cafes selling *calamares a la romana* (squid), dealers selling '*chocolate*' or hashish, stamp dealers at the Sunday-morning market, palmists, artists and tramps, with the odd policeman keeping a watchful eye. The terrace of the Quinze Nits, is a good place from which to watch the proceedings. Also take a look at the street lights which are a youthful work by Gaudí.

### ❽ Santa Monica Art Centre★
**Rambla, 7**
☎ 93 412 22 79
Mon.-Sat. 11am-2pm,
5-8pm, Sun. 11am-3pm
Entry charge.

In 1988 Pinon and Viaplana converted this former 17th-century convent into a contemporary art centre, more or less successfully marrying two styles of architecture. Happily they managed to preserve the cloister. The bookshop is well stocked in design.

### ❾ Boadas★
**Carrer Tallers, 1**
☎ 93 318 88 26
Mon.-Sat. noon-2pm.

This copper and mahogany bar on the corner of the Ramblas is often frequented by politicians and intellectuals. It is reputed to have mixed the best cocktails in the city, *mojitos*, margaritas and dry martinis, since 1933. The founder, Boadas, learnt the secrets of his trade at La Havane, and the barman is of course a real expert.

### ❿ Casa Beethoven★★
**Rambla, 97**
☎ 93 301 48 26
Mon.-Fri. 9am-8pm, Sat.9am-1.30pm, 5-8pm.

Appropriately enough for its name, the owner is a pianist. The wooden shelves and the counter give off the sweetish smell of resin. For nearly a century they have been selling all types of music, from traditional *sardanas* to the bossa nova, rumba, Schubert and, of course, Beethoven.

### ⓫ Xancò★
**Ramblas, 78-80**
☎ 93 318 09 89
Mon.-Sat.
10am-2pm, 4.30-8.30pm.

Time has stood still here at Xancò. Made-to-measure shirts have been produced here since 1820, adapting to changing fashion as the years have passed and carefully arranged on carved wooden shelves. You can have your initials embroidered on them and you can choose from twenty-nine colours in a fine cotton poplin from around 10,000 ptas. When you emerge take a look opposite at the superb shop sign of B. Cuadros at no. 82.

### ⓬ Café de l'Òpera★
**Rambla,74**
☎ 93 302 41 80
Mon.-Sun. 9am-3pm.

This bar opposite the Liceu was established in 1929 on the premises of a former chocolate shop, La Mallorquina, and is open and smoke-filled at all

hours. The Thonet chairs and tarnished mirrors lend it a distinctive atmosphere. In the sixties, it saw gatherings of Latin-American novelists, whose work was avidly consumed by the city. *Tertulias*, lengthy discussions on anything from jazz to alternative medicine, were constantly in full swing. Nowadays, however, it's frequented mainly by tourists.

herbal teas to heal all ills, fragrant essences and a surprisingly wide choice of so-called miracle cures.

### ⑭ Antiga Casa Figueras★★
**Rambla, 83**
☎ 93 301 60 27
**Mon.-Sun. 8.30am-9pm.**

The house of Escribà, heirs to a family of famous Catalan confectioners, is celebrating its 90th anniversary. It still smells as good as ever since the truffles and bars of bitter chocolate are made on the premises. Don't miss the *pastas alimenticias* shop sign and the extraordinary *Modernista* decor – sculpture, mosaics and stained-glass windows, all the applied arts are on display here to welcome all you foodies.

### ⑬ Herbolari Farran★★
**Plaça Reial, 18**
☎ 93 304 20 05
**Mon.-Sat.**
**9.30am-2pm, 4.30-8pm.**

Go along pretty Bacardi passage to this first-rate herbalist's. The fragrant plants and herbs exude health and well-being. You'll find

'Rambla' comes from the Arab word *ramla*, meaning sand. La Rambla follows the course of what was once a river. Until the 14th century it served as the western boundary of the city and marks the site of a 13th-century rampart, which allowed access to the city via the Santa Anna, Portaferissa, Boqueria and Drassana gates. Lampposts at six junctions along the *passeig* mark their position. A mosaic of *azulejos* at the start of Portaferissa street, shows the layout of the old walls.

# L'Eixample: the marvels of Modernisme

At the turn of the century the Eixample, literally 'the extension', became the most prestigious part of the city. Many of its *Modernista* buildings house exclusive shops. The trendy lay siege to *Vinçon* to acquire the latest designer lamps, whilst swarms of eager tourists descend on *Loewe* and re-emerge triumphant, brandishing designer leather goods. Meanwhile, seated on benches in the wide avenues outside, businessmen devour the newspapers, one of the morning's ritual pleasures. It's an affluent and busy district, full of opulence.

## ❶ Passeig de Gràcia★

From 1890 to 1925, Passeig de Gràcia was an upper-middle class residential area. The city's first gas lamps were installed here and it became a fashionable place to walk at turn of the century. The bourgeoisie paraded in their horse-drawn carriages, their children accompanied by Galician nannies. Carnivals alternated with military processions, so there was frequently a festive air.

## ❷ Museu de la Música★★★

**Avinguda. Diagonal, 373**
☎ **93 416 11 57**
**Tue.-Sun. 10am-2pm,
Wed. 5-8pm**
**Entry charge.**

Known as the Palau Quadras, this building was erected by the architect Puig i Cadafalch in 1906. The beautiful staircase and mosaic floor, columns with floral capitals and stone fountain of the entrance hall all add up to a building of great harmony.

The collection of old instruments is particularly rich in guitars and they have an impressive collection of organs too.

### ❸ Casa Milà★★
Provença, 261-265
☎ 93 484 59 95
**Temporary exhibition room**
**Open Mon.-Sun. 10am-8pm**
**Entry charge.**

Gaudí's last, astonishing secular building was built between 1905 and 1910. Known locally as la Pedrera (the quarry), its rippling limestone façade – more sculpture than architecture – was to culminate in a tribute to the Virgin Mary, but his patrons, the Milà family, objected. Gaudí abandoned the project in order to devote all his time and energy to La Sagrada Familia (see p.29). This is still used as an apartment block, but you can gain access to the roof, which is worth doing in order to see the strangely curving chimneys.

### ❹ Manzana de la Discordia★★★
Casa Lleò Morera,
Casa Amatller, Casa Batlló
☎ 93 488 06 66
Passeig de Gràcia
**No tours.**

At the turn of the century each of the great families commissioned the greatest of the city's architects, to erect

suitably grand buildings with which to etch their names in posterity. The clashing styles of these buildings designed between 1898 and 1906, resulted in the name Manzana de la Discordia, or 'Block of Discord'. Architectural styles pre-dating the industrial revolution were used as well as the *Modernista* style (see p. 22). These lavish residences were designed and built on a strictly rectangular grid plan, like pawns on a chess board, as you can see on the map.

### ❺ Casa Calvet★★
Carrer de Casp, 48
**No tours.**

Gaudí's first building and the only one for which he was awarded a prize in 1900. There are several strange things about it, including

three saints' heads provocatively watching passers-by, richly-decorated pulley supports and wrought-iron balustrade projections which soften and round off the rough stonework façade.

### ❻ Fundació Antoni Tàpies★★★
Carrer d'Aragò, 255
☎ 93 487 03 15
**Tue.-Sun. 11am-8pm**
**Entry charge.**

This is the result of the combined genius of two famous Catalan artists. In 1886 the architect Domenech i Montaner designed the Montaner i Simon publishing house, which later became the Antoni Tàpies Foundation. The cast iron and glass open-work exterior is ideal for exhibiting Tàpies' works (see p.27). The building also houses a library and temporary exhibitions.

### ❼ University★
**Gran via de les Corts Catalanes, 585**
**No tours.**

The first university of Catalonia was founded at Lerida in 1300. At the start of the 15th century, King Martín the Humane introduced formalised teaching in the arts and medicine. The university had to move to Cervera in the 18th century, but the present neo-Romanesque building, with an attractive courtyard and gardens, was not built until 1861 by Elies Rogent. The library contains more than two million volumes, manuscripts and priceless early printed books.

### ❽ Happy Books★★
**Carrer de Provenza, 286**
☎ 93 487 30 01
**Mon.-Sat. 9.30am-9pm.**

In such a bustling district, the interior garden of this bookshop is very appealing. At one time or another, all the students from the university come to sit at tables under trees garlanded with little lights to devour Mendoza,

Vázquez Montalbán, Monzo or Pamies, all respected Catalan authors. Try taking a literary break and sip a *horchata* in this tranquil setting.

### ❾ Vinçon★★
**Passeig de Gràcia, 96**
☎ 93 215 60 50
**Mon.-Sat.**
**10am-2pm, 4.30-8.30pm.**

This shop's *Modernista* setting is very characteristic of

L'Eixample, at the turn of the century. In 1929, Vinçon set up this shop selling fine porcelain from his homeland, and then launched into contemporary design. You'll find that everything from key rings to sofas has the stamp of a great designer – Pedro Miralles, Alicia Nunez, Mariscal or Nancy Robbins.

### ❿ Tragaluz restaurant★
**Passatge de la Concepció, 5**
☎ 93 487 06 21
**Every day**
**1.30-4pm, 9pm-1.30am.**

This very fashionable restaurant is a perfect example of its kind. The refined surroundings and muffled atmosphere offer a choice of stylish nouvelle cuisine dishes to match the setting, a turn-of-the-century villa with a very sophisticated designer decor. Choose a mezzanine table for the best view (around 4,000 ptas).

Bar de Vinos, Tapas Japonesas

### ⓫ Antonio Miró★★
**Carrer de Consell de Cent, 349**
☎ 93 487 06 70
**Mon.-Sat. 10am-8.30pm.**

The Barcelona designer
Antonio Miró is also well
known internationally. The
graphic décor of his shop was
designed by Pilar Libano, in
keeping with his elegant silk,
viscose and cotton clothes for
men and women. It is a lesson
in how to be chic without
shocking – women's suits cost
from 70,000 ptas.

### ⓬ Le Café du Centre★★★
**Carrer Girona, 69**
☎ 93 488 11 01
**Mon.-Fri. 7-3am,**
**Sat. 7.30pm-3am.**

During the Republic (1931-
1936), Le Café du Centre
was a very reputable and
distinguished gaming house.
When gambling was
prohibited, it was converted
into a *bodega*, a wine bar
serving a selection of cold
ham and sausages, *embotits*,
and *pa amb tomàquet*, slices
of toasted bread with olive oil
and tomatoes (2,000 ptas).
Ask for a table where *L'Avi*, a
legendary croupier, shuffled
the cards and established his
reputation. Place your bets
please!

### ⓭ Roca Jewellers★★
**Passeig de Gràcia,18**
☎ 93 318 32 66
**Mon.-Fri.**
**9.30am-1.30pm, 4.30-8pm,**
**Sat. (in winter only)**
**10am-1.30pm, 5-8pm.**

The interior of this jeweller's
shop, which is the work of the
architect Josep Lluis Sert, a
friend of Joan Miró, is a
superb example of rationalist
architecture. Space, light and
colour combine with the
furniture to lend the décor
great purity. It's the perfect
setting for a jewellers.

### THE CERDÀ PLAN

When the ramparts
disappeared in 1854
Idelfons Cerdà was given
the task of produc-
ing plans for the
Eixample.
Belonging to the
generation of Proudhon,
Hegel and the Romantic
Movement he planned a
modern, democratic city based
on a grid shape, cut by diagonal
avenues. Work began in 1859
and an elegant and airy new
district was born, with residential
and apartment blocks, gardens
and wide avenues, which quickly
became the area in which to live.

# Ciutadella: a green haven

The Ciutadella park looks inviting enough for a stroll, and in summer provides an escape from the mugginess of the city. Lovers kiss on the boating lake while laughing children chase pigeons along the paths, try out their bikes and greet *Copito de Nieve*, the albino gorilla and zoo mascot. It's an open space filled with light that brightens up the dark, cramped maze of the old districts.

### ❶ Estació de França★★
**Av. Marquès de l'Argentera**
**☎ 93 319 64 16**
**Every day 6am-11.30pm.**

The Estació de França station was built for the 1929 Universal Exhibition by the engineer A. Montaner, and restored in 1992. It was

one of the most modern stations of its time, with metal arches spanning over 30m/100ft overhanging the platforms. Its splendid architecture can still produce some gasps today.

### ❷ Parc de la Ciutadella★
**Three entrances: Pg. Picasso, Pg. Pujades, C. Wellington**
**Every day 10am-5pm in winter, 9.30am-7.30pm in summer.**

On 11 September 1714, the city surrendered to its new king, Philip V of Spain. A section of the Ribera district was razed to the ground (see p. 38) in order to build a stronghold, symbolic of the subjugation of Barcelona by the Bourbons. The fortress was attacked in the 19th century, during a resurgence of Catalan nationalism.

It was demolished in 1868 and the area converted into a park.

### ❸ City Zoo★

Parc de la Ciutadella
☎ 93 225 67 80
Every day 10am-5pm in
winter, 9.30am-7.30pm in
summer
Entry charge.

The Parc Zoològic occupies a
good portion of the south-east
part of the park. Colourful
birds from all over the world,
toucans, macaws and parrots,
marmosets,
dolphins, are
all housed
here, but
the star
exhibit
is Copito
de Nieve
(Snowflake),
the unique albino gorilla.

### ❹ Museu d'Art Modern de Catalunya★★★

Parc de la Ciutadella
☎ 93 319 57 28
Every day except Mon. 10am-
7pm Sun. 10am-2.30pm.
Entry charge.

Housed in the former arsenal,
the museum presents a
marvellous insight into turn-
of-the-century Barcelona. The
collections cover the period
from 1830 to 1930. Look out
for Fortuny, Russinyol, Casas,
Mir and Nonell. If
you're a fan of
*Modernista* and

Noucentista architecture (see
p. 22), visit the room dedicated
to the decorative arts, which
reflects the interior decoration
of the buildings. Gaspar
Homar's precious marquetry
and the rippling lines of Gaudí
chairs delight the eye.

### ❺ Parc de la Ciutadella Umbracle and Hivernacle★★

☎ 93 310 22 91
Café Hivernacle open
Mon.-Fri. 10am-midnight,
Sat.-Sun. 10am-5pm.
This is an English-style park
with two large glass-houses.
One is called the Umbracle,
built in 1883), a combination
of ironwork columns and
beams. It once housed a
botanical school, but now
contains teak deck chairs
where you can lounge and
dream of the tropics. The
other, the Hivernacle, has a
light ironwork structure,
perfect for relaxing on a
balmy summer evening.

### ❻ Arc de Triomf and Museu de Zoologia★★

Passeig Picasso
☎ 93 319 69 12
Tue.-Sun. 10am-2pm
Entry charge.

The Parc de la Ciutadella
staged the Universal

Exhibition of 1888. The Arc de
Triomf was erected to provide
a monumental entrance,
opening out onto a very
fashionable boulevard, the
Passeig San Joan. The café-
restaurant of the Exhibition
is now the site of the Museu
de Zoologia. Designed by
Domenech i Montaner, the
Castell dels Tres Dragons
(Castle of the Three Dragons),
as it came to be known, has
medieval and Moorish
elements. The Zoological
Museum contains displays of
stuffed animals and birds.

### ❼ SET PORTES RESTAURANT★★

Passeig Isabel II,
☎ 93 319 30 33.
Every day 1pm-1am.

An institution and cult restaurant with a visitors' book
that has Che Guevara's signature
alongside that of Manolete, John
Wayne, Garcia Lorca, Miró and
Ava Gardner. The 19th-century
beams lit by rustic lamps are
the ideal setting for a *paella
marinera* or black rice from the
Empordà (around 3,000 ptas).

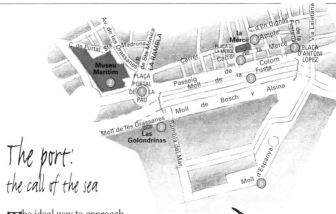

# The port:
## the call of the sea

The ideal way to approach Barcelona is by boat, as in the 19th century. Barcelona's wealth comes from the sea. Until 1900 visitors to Barcelona landed by rowing boat. Nowadays, if you feel like seeing the port, cross the elegant Rambla de Mar footbridge to the Moll d'Espanya, a recent addition to the city. On Sundays, whole families stroll here, proud to be part of the new capital of the Mediterranean now that Barcelona has shown its mettle and resumed its vocation once more.

### ❶ Christopher Colombus Monument★
**Plaça Portal de la Pau**
☎ 93 302 52 24
25 Sep.-30 Mar. Mon.-Fri. 10am-1.30pm, 3.30-6.30pm, Sat.-Sun. 10am-6.30pm, 1 Apr.-31 May Mon.-Fri. 10am-2pm, 3.30-7.30pm, Sat.-Sun. 10am-7.30pm, 1 Jun.-24 Sep. every day 9am-8.30pm. Entry charge.

The 50m/165ft high column was erected for the Universal Exhibition of 1888, in homage to Christopher Columbus. From the top, you can pay your respects to the Genoese (or Catalan, as they say here)

explorer at close range. His finger isn't pointing in the direction of America, but towards the Mediterranean, the source of the city's wealth.

### ❷ Drassanes and Museu Marítim★★
**Avinguda Drassanes**
☎ 93 301 18 71
Tue.-Sun. 10am-7pm
Entry charge.

Ships unique in Europe in terms of size were built here from the 14th to 17th centuries. The industrial activity of the Drassanes, the medieval shipyards, was

prolific. Numerous vessels were launched from its shipyards, from commercial ships to warships. At the Museu Marítim, you can admire the replica of the Royal galley that took part in the Battle of Lepanto (1571). You can also set out on 'The Great Sea Adventure' without too much sea spray, since it's a special film show.

### ❸ Las Golondrinas, la Rambla de Mar★

**Porta de la Pau**
☎ 93 442 31 06
**Departures every 35 minutes Mar.-Oct. every day 11am-8pm, Nov.-Feb. Sat.-Sun. 11am-6pm and weekday mornings. Boarding charge.**

To explore the port at water level, board a *golondrina*, a small boat moored to the quay. You'll be given the history of the harbour, whose first stone was laid in the 15th century. Since 1994, la Rambla de Mar, a swing footbridge in the form of a magnificent metal wave, has been outlined against the sky. It was designed by Viaplana and Pinon.

### ❹ Church of La Mercè and Carrer Ample★

**Plaça de la Mercé**
**Mon.-Sat. 10am-1pm, 6-8.30pm,**
**Sun. 10am-1.30pm, 7-8.30pm.**

In the 18th century this district saw the building of the aristocratic residences on Carrer Ample. You'll have the best view of the Baroque façade of the basilica from the square with its imposing statue of Neptune. The Church would buy back Catalan prisoners from the Barbary pirates. The Virgin

of La Mercè, the city's highly venerated patron saint, is celebrated on 22 and 24 September, with fireworks, giants and *castellers* (see p.16).

### ❺ Carrer de la Mercè and Moll de la Fusta★

Looking for a street with *tapas*? There's *Pulperia* at 16 Carrer de la Mercè, with *patatas bravas* (a potato dish) and fried octopus to whet your

### ❼ CERVANTÈS' HOUSE★★★

**Passeig Colon, 2**
**No tours.**

According to local tradition, no. 2 is nicknamed *Casa Cervantès*. Apparently the writer stayed here during a visit in 1610. The stone façade of the house can be distinguished by its ornate windows. Maybe it was behind one of them that Cervantès imagined *Don Quijote* on the beach of Barceloneta, fighting the White Moon knight.

appetite. *Bodega la Plata* at no. 28. serves local white wine from a *porrò* (see p. 11), accompanied by grilled sardines, which are a real 'must'. If you prefer more trendy places, try the Moll de la Fusta. In the eighties the docks were demolished to create this promenade lined with bars and restaurants. One of the high notes is the sculpture by Roy Lichtenstein (1992), *la Cara de Barcelona* (the face of Barcelona), a colourful creation that stands out against the blue sky.

### ❻ Le Moll d'Espanya★★

**Maremagnum shopping centre**
**Every day 11am-11pm.**
**Aquarium**
☎ 93 221 74 74
**Every day 9.30am-11pm (9pm in winter)**
**Entry charge.**
**Imax ☎ 902 33 22 11**
**Entry charge.**

This is the new place to go on a Sunday to see the natural world. Walk through the aquarium's 80m/260ft transparent tunnel, watch the dozen or so sharks at play, find out about the life of the beaver from the Imax cinema's 360° screen, buy 'organic' cotton shirts from Peru at Natura and a toy for the children at Imaginarium (see p. 91). And finally, treat yourself to a vegetarian lunch.

# From Barceloneta to Port Olímpic: an up-to-date coastline

Since 1992, the slogan *Barcelona oberta al mar* (Barcelona open to the sea) has become a fashionable theme. Town planners have transformed the coastline. Once you practically dined with your feet in the water in the *chiringuitos*, old family eateries that were abruptly torn down. If you're nostalgic for some Barceloneta 'local colour' then head for its central streets. You'll see washing fluttering on balconies, old people out for a breath of fresh air in their slippers, and cafés echoing to cheers as Barça score again.

## ❶ Marina Port Vell★★

The city hasn't always benefited from the sheltered port it has today. Until the 19th century ships had to stay out at sea while small craft transferred their merchandise to the shore. Port Vell is the old port, whose main feature today is the Maremagnum leisure complex of shops and bars. The marina is a recent addition (1992), and the

yachts now add a touch of luxury to one of the oldest industrial parts of the port.

## ❷ Palau de Mar, Museu d'Història Catalunya★★★
Plaça Pau Vila
☎ 93 225 47 00
Tue.-Thu. 10am-7pm,
Fri.-Sat. 10am-8pm,
Sun. 10am-2.30pm.
Entry charge.

The Palau de Mar, part of the 19th-century docks, is an old

warehouse which has recently been given a facelift, but remains a fine example of industrial architecture. These 'general warehouses for trade and commerce' house the new Museum of Catalan History, on two floors. This presents great moments in Catalan history in an educational and entertaining way, through creative displays, films, special effects, interactive screens and hands-on exhibits. Afterwards, you can enjoy something to eat on the terrace of the docks and dream of pirates and buccaneers.

### ❸ Moll dels Pescadors★★
**Cable car closed for restoration Entry charge.**

The fishermen's jetty is only accessible during the fish auctions, when the place becomes a hive of activity from daybreak onwards as the fish wholesalers bid for the best parts of the catch. At night the jetty is lit by the glow from the light of the old beacon (1772). St Sebastiàn's Tower is a familiar sight in the port and forms the terminus for the cable-car, which you can take back to Monjuïc.

### ❹ Barceloneta and its beach★★
Barceloneta is home to part of the city's folklore. It was

created in the 18th century, when the Ribera (see p. 38) was razed to the ground to build the Ciutadella (see p. 52). Its inhabitants had to wait until 1753 to be re-housed in Barceloneta. It has retained the charm of some of the old mediterranean cities – you could be in Palermo or Naples. The people of Barcelona bathed at the Banos St Sebastiàn and the Banos Orientales at the turn of the Century. Today, there is a five-kilometre stretch of palm-fringed beach for bathers and sun-worshippers.

### ❺ Church of St Miquel del Port★
**Every day 7am-1.45pm, 4.30-8pm.**

This church was built when Barceloneta was in its infancy, in 1753, in honour of St Miquel, Barceloneta's patron saint. Its façade is a fine example of Baroque architecture. In summer, it's delightfully cool and children play football outside in the square to cries of 'Força Barça'.

### ❻ Passeig Marítim, water tower and gasometer tower★
Passeig Marítim links 18th-century Barceloneta with the new Port Olímpic. As you walk along, you'll discover what remains of the area's industrial past. The *Modernista* silhouette of the Water Tower by J.Domenech Estapà, built in 1906 is very striking and the structure of the former gasometer will soon be the centrepiece of a park.

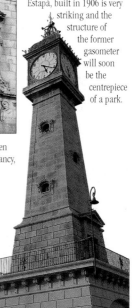

### **7** Port Olímpic and Whale by Frank Gehry★★

The designer restaurants of Port Olímpic have replaced the cheaper, unassuming restaurants which lined the shore just a few years ago. It is quite usual to see several generations gather round a table for a family meal on Sunday, then take a stroll along the quays in the afternoon. A vast bronze whale is 'beached' here. Its 50m/165ft skeleton was designed by the architect Frank Gehry. In 1992 during the Barcelona Olympic Games, the watersport events were started from Port Olímpic.

### **8** Arts Hotel★
**Carrer de la Marina 19-21**
**☎ 93 221 10 00.**

Two towers dominate Port Olímpic. One of them,

designed by Ortiz i Leon, houses Mapfre Insurance, the second is the luxurious Arts-Ritz-Carlton hotel. Its Terraza bar (every day 11am-2am) has one of the best views of Frank Gehry's whale, not to mention an overview of the port itself. The hotel's choice of *puros* (cigars) and *cavas* (local champagne) cocktails is quite unique.

For 'designer *tapas*' go to Goyescas, the hotel restaurant (open every day 1-4pm, 8pm-2am).

### **9** Nova Icària★

Nova Icària is the latest redevelopment project for 130 hectares/320 acres of coastline. It has appropriated part of the Poble Nou, the 'Catalan Manchester' of the 19th century, where only a few factory chimneys remain as a reminder of the area's industrial past. In the 1990s, architects took over, with the backing of property developers, to invent the city of the future and create the Olympic Village. Athletes were housed here during the 1992 Olympic Games. Manuel Vázquez Montalbán, the writer, is quoted as saying,

*'The new Olympic Village is like an Oxford graduate playing cricket at the doors of the Bronx'.*

### **10** Baja Beach Club★★★
**Passeig Marítim**
**☎ 93 225 91 00**
**Summer every day**
**noon-5am**
**Winter Thu.-Sun. noon-5am.**

One of the most recent of the new bars which go in and out of fashion so quickly, the Beach Club is the latest trendy venue, a disco, café and restaurant all rolled into one. It features rather vulgar shows and sexy waitresses, so consider yourself warned! The menu is American-style. You really come here more for the entertainment than for the food.

and the beer is still draught. The open-plan kitchen is clearly visible to the diners who can see the delicious dishes being prepared in front of them (see p. 10).

*Sarsuela* (Catalan fish stew) was invented here and Casa Solé has been serving delicious traditional dishes ever since.

### ⓫ Two open-air sculptures★★★

The streets and squares of Barcelona include over 430 monuments. Many of them were erected during the first

(see p. 10).

### ⓬ L'Antiga Casa Solé★★

**Carrer Sant Carles, 4**
☎ 93 221 50 12
Tue.-Sun. lunchtime
1-4pm, 8-11pm.

This port bistrot, which opened in 1903, still has four of its original marble tables. Its waiters still wear white jackets

thirty years of the 20th century, but their number multiplied in the eighties and nineties. One example from what you might term this open-air museum is Antoni Llena's *David and Goliath* (1993). Another is by Rebecca Horn. Her sculpture *Hommage to Barceloneta* (1992) is to be found on the beach. It evokes the *chiringuitos*, the little kiosks selling food which have since vanished.

## LOS CHIRINGUITOS

Since 1941, fishermen's families have prepared simple meals for bathers on the beach at Barceloneta, cooked in *chiringuitos*, little kiosks. These proliferated in the San Sebastiàn and Los Orientales areas, but were only open in summer. However, in 1991, the kiosks sadly were demolished, and part of the city's folklore disappeared along with them.

# Diagonal Pedralbes: the city heights

Mountains and plains, sky and sea, Pyrenees and Mediterranean, this duality defines the Catalan country and its capital. For centuries the lure of a vista inland or over the sea has drawn the people of Barcelona to its upper levels. Monasteries, villas, gardens and parks are dotted around the hillsides. In summer the light breezes are heaven-sent and open-air cafes are much in demand.

### ❶ Jardíns and Palau de Pedralbes★★
Avinguda Diagonal, 686
Museu de les Arts Decoratives
☎ 93 280 50 24
Museu de Ceràmica
☎ 93 280 16 21
Tue.-Sun. 10am-3pm
Joint ticket.

This royal residence was built in the 1920s on land that once belonged to Don Güell. It houses the Museu de les Arts Decoratives and Museu de Ceràmica. There are unique pieces with enamel decoration by Artigas, Miró and Picasso.

### ❷ Monestir de Pedralbes★★
Baixada Monestir, 9
☎ 93 203 92 82
Tue.-Sun. 10am-2pm
Entry charge.

This is one of the most attractive walks in the city. The name Pedralbes probably comes from the Latin *petras Albas* (white stone). Commissioned around 650 years ago by Elisende de Montcada, wife of Jaume II, the church was consecrated in 1327. On her husband's death the queen retreated to the

monastery surrounded by her court. The three-storey cloisters are evocative of 600 years of convent life, and are a fine illustration of Catalan Gothic architecture. In St Michael's

chapel, the murals of Ferrer Bassa are evidence of the close ties between the Italians and Catalans in the 14th century.

## ❸ Thyssen-Bornemisza Collection★★★
Baixada Monestir, 9
☎ 93 280 14 34
Tue.-Sun. 10am-2pm
Entry charge.

Since 1993, the Monastery of Pedralbes has exhibited part of the Thyssen-Bornemisza Collection. Former dormitories of the St Clare of Assisi order of nuns were converted to house the collection, evidence of the close links between medieval Italy and Catalonia. It features 13th to 18th-century paintings from European Schools. If you're short of time, the highlights are Fra Angelico's *Virgin of Humility*, Titian's *Virgin and Child*, Tintoretto's *Portrait of the Senator*, Ruysdaël's *Seascape*, Canaletto's *Bucentaure* and Guardi's *St Mark's Square*.

## ❹ Entrance to the Finca Güell★★
Avinguda Pedralbes, 7.

The main gate and entrance pavilions of the Finca Güell by Gaudí once again demonstrate his tireless ornamental inventiveness. The Moorish caretaker's lodge could be mistaken for a sultan's harem, and the dragon standing guard is undoubtedly a Catalan Art Nouveau wrought-iron masterpiece, with

menacing jaws ready to discourage any unwanted visitors. But don't let it put you off!

## ❺ Avinguda Diagonal★
This avenue crosses the city from east to west. It was planned in 1859, like

L'Eixample (see p. 48). The top of the avenue is the business centre, with luxury hotels, insurance companies, large department stores (Illa and Corte Inglès, see p.92) and banks. The logo designed by Miró is displayed on the Caixa de Pensions façade. This 5-pointed star is the emblem of one of the most powerful banking organisations in Europe. Diagonal is now being extended to the sea.

## ❻ THE ASCENT OF THE TIBIDABO★★★
If you'd like to see some views, take a taxi to the foot of the Tibidabo (10 minutes from Pedralbes). Then take the *tramvía blau*, one of the last vestiges of Barcelona's tram system. This 'electric' ascent to the summit gives you the opportunity to admire the *Modernista* villas built by the Barcelona middle classes at the turn of the century. Every respectable family had a *torre* (villa) in the countryside. At the end of the journey, sit at a table on the terrace of the Venta, a quaint Moorish open-air café.

# Montjuïc: the reclaimed hill

Montjuïc was named after the Jewish community that once lived here. Given a costly facelift for the 1992 Olympic Games, the people of Barcelona now come for some fresh air, though there's a lot to do and see. You can have a picnic, stroll along the terraces of the Miró Foundation, place a bet at the Plaça d'Espanya greyhound track, or, if you really must, go for a jog – the marathon entrance to the Olympic stadium isn't far away.

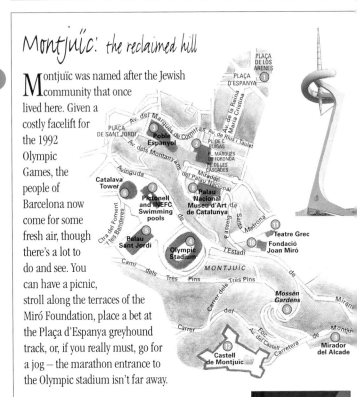

### ❶ Carrer de Llancà and Plaça de los Arenes★★

**Gran via Corts Catalanes, 385**
**☎ 93 325 46 08**
**Open Mon., Fri., Sat., Sun.**
**11am-2pm, 5-9pm,**
**Tue. Wed. and Thu. 5-9pm**
**Free entry.**

The Plaça d'Espanya, at the site of a former crossroads, was built for the 1929 Universal Exhibition (see p.65). At its centre is an ornate fountain by J.M. Jujol, a colleague of Gaudí, which represents the rivers of the Iberian Peninsula. To the north lies the now-disused 'neo-Moorish' bull-ring of

1899. Catalans despise the bull-fighting lifestyle of Madrid preferring the neighbouring greyhound-racing track. To each his own!

### ❷ Mies Van der Rohe Pavilion★★

**Av. del Marquès de Comillas**
**☎ 93 423 40 16**
**Every day 10am-6pm**
**in summer until 8pm.**
**Entry charge.**

The Pavello d'Alemanya lies at the foot of the Montjuïc. It was destroyed at the end

of the 1929 Universal Exhibition, but then was reconstructed in 1986. It has a simple, abstract shape, made of marble, stone, onyx and glass.

### ❸ Poble Espanyol★

**Av. del Marquès de Comillas**
**☎ 93 325 78 66**
**Mon. 9am-8pm, Tue.-Thu. 9am-2pm, Fri.-Sat. 9am-4pm, Sun. 9am-midnight**
**Entry charge.**

This 'Spanish Village' was initially conceived for visitors to the 1929 Universal Exhibition as a lightning tour of Spain, but is still just as popular today, representing as it does the diversity of Spanish regional architecture. Folk crafts are on sale in the village and there are restaurants serving regional dishes. Go to the top of the Torres de Avila to the bar of the same name (see p.119) for an amazing view.

### ❹ Olympic Stadium and Galería★

**Avinguda de l'Estadi Stadium every day 10am-6pm (8pm in summer). Entry free at Puerta Maraton Galería**
**☎ 93 426 06 60**
**Apr.-Jun. Tue.-Sun. 10am-2pm, 4-7pm, Oct.-Mar. Tue.-Fri. 10am-1pm, 4-6pm, Sat.-Sun. 10am-2pm, Jul.-Sep. Tue.-Sun. 10am-2pm, 4-8pm**
**Entry charge at South Gate.**

The walls by Pere Domenech date from 1929, and the façade and equestrian sculptures by Gargallo have also been preserved. Just imagine some 60,000 spectators in full voice cheering the athletes on to victory. In the gallery you can see the costumes created by Els Comedians for the Olympic ceremonies.

### ❺ Palau Sant Jordi ★★★

**Avinguda de l'Estadi**
**☎ 93 426 20 89**
**Sat.-Sun. 10am-6pm.**
**Free entry to the Olympic Esplanade.**

The Japanese Arata Isozaki made use of state-of-the-art technology when designing the site of the 1992 gymnastics events. However, athletes have been supplanted by showbiz, and rock concerts now call the tune.

At sunset, Miyawaki's sculptures create a beautiful graphic effect – a forest of metallic trees, futuristic creations, are outlined against the sky.

### ❻ Calatrava Tower ★★

**Plaça Europa**
**Free entry.**

This space-age telecommunications tower is the elegant counterpoint of the Palau Sant Jordi. It was designed by Santiago Calatrava and dominates the skyline, pointing the way to new horizons.

### ❼ Picornell Swimming pools and INEFC★
Avinguda de l'Estadi.

The swimming-pool complex was remodelled for the Olympic competitions and is named after Bernat Picornell, the Catalan swimming pioneer. It rubs shoulders with the neo-Classical building of the Institut Nacional de Educació Fisica de Catalunya (INEFC). The latter, built round a cloister, is typical of its Catalan designer, Ricardo Bofill. The way in is through a portico with Doric columns, like an ancient Greek temple – very impressive, but not particularly innovative. The light-coloured building stands out against a radiant blue sky, once again to grandiose effect.

### ❽ Museu Nacional d'Art de Catalunya, MNAC★★
Parc de Montjuïc
☎ 93 423 71 99
Every day except Mon.
10am-7pm, Thu. 10am-9pm,
Sun. 10am-2.30pm
Entry charge.

Symbol of the 1929 Exhibition and recently restored by Gae Aulenti, the former National Palace has housed collections of Catalan art since 1934. Don't miss the superb Roman and Gothic collections. There are remarkable 12th-century frescoes by Urgell and Taüll. This, the best of the art museums in Barcelona, is being renovated and reorganised to bring together all the city's art collections under one roof. Work will not be completed until 2001.

### ❾ Mirador de l'Alcalde and Mossen Gardens Costa i Llobrera
Plaça del Mirador
Free entry.

Opposite the entrance to the amusement park and esplanade, this provides one of the most enjoyable views of the port. The ground is a collage of ceramic fragments and bottle bases. A sculpture by Subirachs pays 'Homage to Barcelona'. Down below, the Mossen Gardens go cascading down to the port.

### ❿ Fondació Joan Miró★★★
Parc Montjuïc
☎ 93 329 19 08
Tue.-Sat. 11am-7pm
(8pm Jul.-Sep.), Thu. until
9.30pm, Sun. 10.30am-
2.30pm. Entry charge.

This beautiful white building housing the works of Joan Miró was opened in 1975. Designed by his friend Josep Lluis Sert, it is in a magical setting in the gardens overlooking the city. The works – paintings, sculptures, tapestries and graphics – cover the period 1914-1978 and were donated by Miró himself. There is a restaurant and bookshop.

## ⑪ Teatre Grec★
**Passeig de l'Exposicio.**

This reproduction of a Greek theatre was installed in a disused quarry below the Miró Foundation, once again for the 1929 Exhibition. The quarry's sandstone has been used to build the city since Roman times. In the Middle Ages porters carried the stone down from Montjuïc for the building of Santa Maria del Mar free of charge. The theatre is now

used during the city's cultural festival held in summer. If you can get tickets, an evening spent in this extraordinary place watching a performance as the sun sets, is just magical.

## ⑫ Castell de Montjuïc and Military Museum
**Summit of Montjuïc Hill**
☎ **93 329 86 13**
**Open every day except Mon. 9.30am-7.30pm Entry charge.**

The castle of Montjuïc has witnessed some very bloody times. Designed in 1751 by the engineer Cermeno, it is in the shape of a star. The city was bombarded from the castle in the 1942 rebellion and five prisoners were executed here by firing squad in 1896, as were Falangists during the Civil War. It has housed the Museu Militar (military

In May 1929, Alphonse XIII inaugurated the Universal Exhibition. It was a showcase for the dictatorship of Primo de Rivera, and only survived him by a few weeks. Most of the buildings you'll see on the hillsides are former pavilions that have been turned into museums or theatres. The Mercat dels Flors theatre, for example, is a strange and ghostly place, but worth a detour.

history museum) since 1960 which has fine collections of weaponry, armour, uniforms and maps, as well as portraits of the counts and kings of Catalonia.

# Sitges:
## a short hop to the beach

The fine sandy beaches of the Costa Daurada lie between Barcelona and Tarragona. The seaside resort of Sitges has been spared by developers and still retains the elegant character of a turn-of-the century holiday resort, with several *Modernista* villas, a shady palm-fringed *passeig* (promenade), and a church with a pink façade. The resort is perhaps best-known for its pulsating nightlife and is also a popular gay holiday destination. Trains to Sitges go from Passeig de Gràcia station.

### ❶ Church square and Passeig de la Ribera★★★

The origins of this once sleepy fishing port are steeped in history. It is said to have been an ancient site and the maritime outlet for the mountain city of Oderdola.

The name Sitges is of Iberian origin and means 'silos' and it is certainly true that stocks of grain have been discovered in hollows carved out of the rock. From the 17th-century church square

you can see the promenade which runs the length of the *Platja d'or*.

### ❷ Museu Cau Ferrat★★

**Carrer Fonollar,**
☎ **93 894 03 64**
**Tue.-Fri. 9.30am-2pm, 4-6pm in winter, 8pm in summer, Sat. 9.30am-2pm, 4-8pm, Sun. 9.30am-2pm. Joint ticket for the three museums**

In 1893, the astonishing artist and writer Santiago Rusiñol acquired a fisherman's cottage and set up his studio there. His collections of wrought-iron work, ceramics and Catalan furniture were

bequeathed to the city by his widow. See the two works by El Greco that Rusiñol paraded through the streets to parody the Easter procession, and paintings by Picasso, Ramon Casas and Nonell.

### 3 Museu Maricel★
See Cau Ferrat.

The former city hospital houses a collection of valuable Spanish works of art donated by a collector. The Gothic rooms contain altar-pieces with gold backgrounds and multi-coloured carved wooden sculptures. The entrance hall decorated by Josep Maria Sert (1874-1945), painter of theatrical frescoes and the husband of Mysia, the muse of the Ballets Russes, is a curiosity. On the top floor the Roig collection contains model ships and musical instruments.

### 4 Le Museu Romàntic★
C. San Gaudenci, 1
☎ 93 894 29 69
See above.

This former residence of the Llopis family dates from 1793. The furniture of the period has been preserved, as have the murals

by Pau Rigalt tracing the life of the city in the late 18th century. It shows the life of a bourgois family in the 18th and 19th centuries. There is also a collection of delicate old dolls, with pretty hats, little bags, muffs and parasols.

### 5 and 6 Hotel-Restaurant El Xalet★★
Carrer Isla de Cuba, 35
☎ 93 811 00 70. Apr.-Oct.,
Every day 1-2.30pm, 8-11pm.

The architect Buigas built this *Modernista* villa in the 19th century. When the *Indianos* – residents who had made their fortune abroad at the end of the 19th

### SANTIAGO RUSIÑOL (1861-1931)

Born of a middle-class family that had made its fortune during the industrial revolution, Rusiñol preferred the Bohemian lifestyle to that of his own class. A fervent Catalan, he travelled abroad regularly and during his stays in Paris cultivated friendships with the painters of Montmartre. He also helped many artists from Barcelona to become known. From 1892 to 1899, Rusiñol organised the *Festes Modernistes*, artistic gatherings of music, painting, sculpture and dance and Sitges became a *Mecca del Modernismo*, or Mecca of Modernism.

century – returned to the country, they wanted to build luxurious residences. Sitges has a good number of these mansions. Entering the dining room of the El Xalet is like stepping back in time. You feel as if you should be taking part in a Merchant-Ivory film. Try some of the delicious home cooking prepared by the proprietor (around 25,000 ptas). A double room costs around 9,000 ptas.

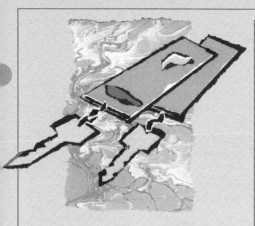

# Rooms and restaurants
## Practicalities

## HOTELS

The city lacked luxury hotels before 1992, but since the Olympic Games it has had a good range of accommodation, with more than 150 hotels meeting the needs of its visitors. If you choose a hotel with sea views, you'll probably find it is in a quiet district, but a long way from the centre. On the other hand, the city centre is noisy and so it's best to ask for a room overlooking a courtyard and there may be a long walk to the hotel as many of them are inaccessible by car.

## RATES AND CONDITIONS

The hotels listed in this guide are divided into four categories. The top three categories include phone, TV and en-suite bathroom; the fourth is more basic. In general, breakfast isn't included in the price of the room. A supplement is also charged for extra beds for children. There's no distinction between smoking and non-smoking rooms.

Rates for a double room before tax:

★★★★★ from 43,000 to 26,000 ptas.

★★★★ from 27,000 to 13,500 ptas.

★★★ from 12,000 to 9,000 ptas.

★★ from 8,000 to 6,000 ptas.

You will be charged an additional 7% tax (*IVA*) per night per room.

If you'd like the complete list of hotels in Barcelona,

## 'WEEKEND' RATES TO LOOK OUT FOR

Many hotels also operate the *'fin de semana'* price, or 'week-end' rate, which is extremely advantageous, since it allows you a discount of up to 50 % of the normal price. It's in your interest to select a higher-category hotel that grants this discount because you'll pay the same price as for an average hotel that doesn't. Always ask at the time of booking. You can also obtain information from:

**Tourist Information Office**: 149, Plaça de Catalunya 17-S
☎ 93 304 32 32
🖶 93 304 32 26
(open every day 9am-9pm)

**Town Hall**: Plaça San Jaume (inside the Ajuntament building)
(open every day 10am to 2pm)

This organisation is responsible for booking your hotel at the *'fin de semana'* rates (operating in 35 selected hotels) and providing you with a BIP (Barcelona Important Person) card, which gives you discounts at restaurants, museums, shows, car hire firms, etc. The advantageous *'fin de semana'* prices operate throughout the year at the week-end (Fri.-Sun.), and every day from 21 June to 11 September, and are definitely worth looking out for. There's no need to send payment in advance – you pay the hotel direct. The rates given below are before tax per person for a double room

Category A (★★★★★): 9,450 ptas

Category B (★★★★): 6,950 ptas

Category C and D (★★★★) and (★★★): 4,950 to 3,950 ptas

### WHEN DO WE EAT?

Spain has its own special mealtimes, with lunch served from 1.30 to 4pm and dinner from 9 or 10 to 11.30pm. Don't arrive too early or you'll come across the staff having their meals.

Nearly all restaurants accept credit cards. A tip isn't mandatory and is never included on the bill in Spain. It's thoughtful to leave 200-300 ptas but anything more is considered excessive.

contact the Barcelona Hotels Association:
Via Laietana 47 (08003),
☎ 93 301 62 40
🖷 93 301 42 92.

You can make reservations in advance by phone or fax. You won't usually be asked for a deposit. However, you're room won't be ready until noon at the earliest.

## RESTAURANTS

Catalan cuisine tends to be fairly substantial and nourishing, but is not afraid of mixing flavours, so you will find savoury dishes flavoured with nuts and fruit. As you may imagine from its proximity to the sea, fish and seafood figure heavily in restaurant menus, but meat is also good here. There are essentially three types of eating establishment, the *restaurante* (*restaurant* in Catalan), the *cafeterîa*, which tends to be cheaper than the restaurants, plus of course you can also order snacks in bars. Most restaurants will have a *menú del dia*, or daily set menu. *Tapas* are small dishes of food, which used to be served free with drinks, but for which you now have to pay. *Raciones* are really just bigger portions of *tapas*. A *bodegas* (literally 'cellar'), *cerveceria* (*cervesseria* in Catalan), *tasca* (*tasques*) and *taberna* are all types of bar (see also p. 13).

In summer, you'll be well advised to make for the port or high parts of the city (Tibidabo) to benefit from the least breeze, though there are also many shaded terraces in the city centre. Generally speaking, you don't need to book in advance, unless you decide to visit one of the trendiest restaurants, in which case, you can ask your hotel receptionist to book for you. There's no formal dress code and you can wear whatever you like – a tie isn't compulsory anywhere. However, the people of Barcelona always make every effort to look their best.

# HOTELS

## Port Olímpic

### Arts Barcelona★★★★★

C. Marina, 19-21, (08005)
☎ 93 221 10 00
Metro Ciutadella
Vila Olímpica.

A hotel beside the sea where businessmen and others find elegant hi-tech rooms and suites with an uninterrupted view of the bay and Port Olímpic. **Bar Terraza** and swimming pool to top up your suntan.

## Eixample

### Claris★★★★★

Carrer Pau Claris, 150 (08009)
☎ 93 487 62 62
Metro Urquinaona

The former palace of the Counts of Vedruna appeals particularly to travellers who appreciate its collection of Egyptian artefacts. Each of its 120 rooms is decorated with antiques, paintings and 17th-century English or *Modernista* furniture. There is a private bar.

### Ritz★★★★★

Gran via de les Corts Catalanes, 668 (08010)
☎ 93 318 52 00
Metro Urquinaona.

A delightful place to spend an evening, where Salvador Dali once demanded a suite for the statue of his horse. A special weekend offer (subject to availability) at this charming, traditional hotel is temptation enough. True to its reputation, a very luxurious hotel.

### Alexandra★★★★

Carrer Mallorca, 251 (08008)
☎ 93 476 71 66
Metro Diagonal.

A convenient place to stay close to the city's shops, with 75 wood-decorated designer rooms. A room overlooking the courtyard will give you an idea of the magnificence of the houses in l'Eixample.

*The astonishing façade of the Claris hotel.*

### Condes de Barcelona★★★★

Pg de Gràcia, 73-75 (08008)
☎ 93 488 22 00
Metro Diagonal.

This *Modernista* building has been brilliantly renovated, preserving the classical Romano-Moorish stairwell and you will receive a courteous welcome. Ask for a room overlooking the garden at the back of the hotel if you're looking for peace and quiet during your stay.

### Duques de Bergara★★★★

Carrer Bergara, 11 (08002)
☎ 93 301 51 51
Metro Catalunya.

You'll love this turn-of-the-century former private mansion, just a stone's throw from Plaça de Catalunya, especially the sumptuous marble entrance and staircase. The convenient car park is a bonus.

### Gran Hotel Havana★★★★

Gran via de les Corts Catalanes, 647 (08010)
☎ 93 412 11 15
Metro Girona.

The hotel's turn-of-the-century façade is reminiscent of the grand hotels of the seaside resorts of San Sebastian. The 145 rooms, all luxurious, are provided with every comfort – satellite television, air-conditioning, safe, etc. Centrally located and ideal if you like shopping.

## St Moritz★★★★

**C. Diputaciò, 262 (08007)**
**☎ 93 412 15 00**
**Metro Passeig de Gràcia.**

A very central hotel with an interior garden that's a bonus in summer. The neo-Classical façade is impressive, as is the size of the rooms equipped with satellite television. The service is attentive and there's a fitness centre if you have enough energy left after shopping in the neighbouring *passeig*.

### Barrio Gòtico

## Colon★★★★

**Avinguda Catedral, 7**
**(08002)**
**☎ 93 301 14 04**
**Metro Jaume I.**

A hotel frequented by Miró opposite the cathedral. Ask for a room with a balcony overlooking the square so that you can follow the movements of the Sunday sardanas (Catalan dancing). Its exceptional location is ideal for exploring the Barrio Gotico.

## Regencia Colon★★★

**Carrer Sagristans, 13-17**
**(08002)**
**☎ 93 318 98 58**
**Metro Jaume I.**

This hotel a stone's throw from the cathedral is less luxurious than the *Colon* (see above) but has the advantage of being in a quiet pedestrian area. It's a good place to come as a family – children can play in the cathedral square.

## Metropol★★★

**Carrer Ample, 31, (08002)**
**☎ 93 310 51 00**
**Metro Jaume I.**

Near Port Vell and at the lower end of the Barrio Gotico, this hotel offers unbeatable value for money. The foyer has retained the character of a private town house, and the rooms are small but secluded. An opportunity you won't want to miss.

## Nouvel★★★

**Carrer Santa Anna, 20 (08002)**
**☎ 93 301 82 74**
**Metro Catalunya.**

The *Modernista* setting of this hotel, a small street in the Barrio Gotico, isn't lacking in charm. Its carved ceilings, old *azulejos* and elegant stairwell make it a delightful place to stay for visitors particularly interested in authentic Art Deco.

## Jardi★★★

**Plaça Sant Josep Oriol, 1**
**(08001)**
**☎ 93 301 59 00**
**Metro Liceu.**

The Jardi is wonderfully located in the beating heart of the city, the Plaça del Pi pedestrian area. The rooms overlook pine trees and street entertainers of all kinds. It's a small but reasonably-priced hotel and our favourite in this category.

### Diagonal

## Rey Juan Carlos I★★★★★

**Av. Diagonal, 661 (08028)**
**☎ 93 448 08 08**
**Metro Zona Universitaria.**

This was the last hotel to open in 1992 and heads of state from around the world stayed here during the Olympic Games. Its cavernous foyer is impressive, and the 412 rooms are arranged round it as if it were a liner. The hotel's distance from the city centre means it has room for gardens, terraces and a pool.

### Gran Derby★★★★

**Carrer Loreto, 28 (08029)**
☎ 93 322 20 62
**Metro Entença.**

To judge from the brick façade, you'd think you were in Chelsea in London, yet the delightful sunlit garden leaves you in little doubt – you are indeed in Barcelona, near the Turò Park district, with its luxurious shop windows. The hotel has ultramodern split-level rooms and staff will go out of their way to hire cars, and book tickets for concerts and excursions to Montserrat for you.

an original way, has given each of its ninety rooms a distinctive touch – antique dealers, designers and young artists were involved. Very good location, but no car park.

### Citadines★★★

**La Rambla, 122 (08002)**
☎ 93 270 11 11
**Metro Catalunya.**

If you want to feel at home, this apartment hotel is the place for you. Each apartment is equipped with everything you might need. If you have inadvertently forgotten the

## Ramblas

### Rivoli Ramblas★★★★

**La Rambla, 128 (08002)**
☎ 93 302 66 43
**Metro Catalunya.**

At the top of the Ramblas, this thirties building, restored in

baby's bottle warmer, or your toothbrush, just call reception who will come to the rescue. Ideal for families.

### Mercure Barcelona Rambla★★★

**La Rambla, 124 (08002)**
☎ 93 412 04 04
**Metro Catalunya.**

In the heart of the Ramblas, the hotel is a strategic starting point for your walks in the Barrio Gotico and Raval. There are 76 convenient rooms behind the turn-of-the-century facade, and a foyer with a new designer look. Very friendly reception.

## Raval

### Sant Agusti★★★

**Plaça Sant Agusti, 3 (08001)**
☎ 93 318 16 58
**Metro Liceu.**

In a shady, peaceful square close to the Ramblas, the Sant Agusti is situated beside St Augustine's church. Ask for the attic rooms with exposed beams, which are quite delightful. There's a handy car park in the area too.

### España★★

**Carrer Sant Pau, 9 (08001)**
☎ 93 318 17 58
**Metro Liceu.**

To fans of Art Nouveau, the dining rooms designed by Domenech i Montaner are quite irresistible. Set in the heart of the Barrio Chino, the España keeps alive memories of a bygone age – but the décor in the dining room is really more memorable than the food. The bedrooms are spacious and comfortable. Ask for a room overlooking the lovely indoor patio if possible.

## Sitges

### San Sebastian★★★★

**Port Alegre, 53 (08870)**
☎ 93 894 86 76.

Opposite the small bay of San Sebastian, the hotel's fifty-one spruce rooms are both pleasant and practical. With the sunny terrace inviting you to relax and enjoy life, it's just the place to satisfy your longing for idleness and the beach (see p. 66-67).

### El Xalet★★

**Carrer Isla de Cuba, 35 (08870)**
☎ 93 811 00 70.

A beautifully preserved *Modernista* villa set in a luxuriant garden with a pool. The ten rooms are furnished with a medley of furniture. The friendly welcome and food from the market lovingly prepared by the owner are sure to please those seeking a quiet setting.

### Romàntic★★

**Carrer Sant Isidre, 33 (08870)**
☎ 93 894 83 75
**Closed in winter .**

An ardent admirer of the turn-of-the-century style saved three *Modernista* houses to create this hotel. Visitors particularly enjoy sitting on the patio planted with palm trees, and the owner enjoys sharing his nostalgia for Modernisme. Ask for a room with a balcony overlooking the garden for the peace and quiet, and the view.

*Hotel Romàntic*

# RESTAURANTS

## Barrio Gòtico

### Hostal El Pintor★★

Carrer St Honorat, 7
☎ 93 301 40 65
Metro Jaume I
Open every day except Sun. eve.

This hotel is pleasantly situated behind the cathedral, with the emphasis on trendy decor – exposed bricks and beams and gleaming floor-tiles. Traditional Catalan cuisine – asparagus with marinated salmon, and hake with leeks grilled the old-fashioned way.

### El Gran Café★

Avinyò, 9
☎ 93 318 79 86
Metro Liceu
Closed Sun. and pub. hols.

El Gran Café's copper coffee percolator, black and white checked floor tiles, bistrot tables and starched tablecloths, put you in mind of fin-de-siècle Paris. Senor Ramon will be only to pleased to show you his connoisseur's wine cellar (bodega), if you ask him. The set lunch is 1,200 ptas.

### Pou Dols★★

Baixada de Sant Miquel, 6
☎ 93 412 05 79
Open Mon.-Sat.

Pou Dols menu is varied and delicious – consommé with

liver mousse, sardine tart with young garlic, white fish with parmesan, and boned pig's trotters with artichokes. With an inventive menu and a sober decor by Starck and Maurer, this is currently a very popular place. After sampling some of these gourmet dishes you will doubtless be added to its list of fans. Not far from the *Ajuntamient* (Town Hall). Allow around 4,000 ptas per person.

## Port and Barceloneta

### Els Pescadors★★★

Plaça Prim, 1
☎ 93 225 20 18
Metro Poble Nou
Open every day.

This terrace beyond the Olympic Village is a delightful place to enjoy the mild air. Opt for the marble-tabled 'antigua' room rather than the more impersonal 'moderna', and try oven-grilled peppers,

black rice with ink, and cod with honey.

### Barceloneta★★

L'Escar, 22 Moll dels Pescadors
☎ 93 221 21 11
Metro Barceloneta
Open every day.

For armchair sailors. Wood, rope and coarse sail-cloth create a nautical atmosphere in this fashionable restaurant overlooking Port Vell. Picture windows, duckboards, wood panelling and red and blue striped canvas tablecloths help to whet the appetite as surely as the sea air.

### Cal Pinxo★★

Baluard, 124
Platja Barceloneta
☎ 93 221 50 28
Metro Barceloneta
Open every day.

With *chiringuitos* (see p. 59) a thing of the past, the Cal

Pinxo restaurant carries on the tradition of the kiosks and fishermen's restaurants, serving *fideus a la cassola*, *paella* with pasta, *mariscos*, seafood and monkfish in *cazuela* with aïlloli sauce.

## Carballeira★★

Reina Cristina 3
☎ 93 310 10 06
Metro Barceloneta
Closed Sun. eve., Mon. and public holidays.

An excellent fish restaurant that makes no concessions to fashion. Plenty of local colour, with portholes, model ships and turtles – an endearing popular classic according to many, an affront according to others. Judge for yourself!

## Reial Club Marítim★★

Moll d'Espanya,
☎ 93 221 62 56
Metro Barceloneta
Closed Sun. eve.

Turning its back on the hi-tech Maremagnum, this little place is like an officers' club from another era. The view of the overhead bridge, *Rambla de Mar*, and the steamers

setting off for the islands only adds to the culinary delights – bass in rosemary, fish soup and fresh pasta with prawns.

## The city heights

### A Contraluz ★★

Milanesado, 19 (not on map)
(via Augusta esq. Dr Roux)
☎ 93 203 06 58
Take a taxi
Open every day.

The roomy setting and summer terrace of this latest Tragaluz restaurant (see p. 50) will make you forget all about the city. Try the delicious risotto with boletus mushrooms, foie gras with baby onions, or potato and vine-leaf puffs. As in most restaurants here, you can sample this tasty Catalan cuisine more cheaply from the lunch menu (2,300 ptas).

### Can Travi Nou★★

Antic Cami de Sant Cebrià
☎ 93 428 03 01
Take a taxi
Closed Sun. eve.

This Catalan property in the city heights has the look of a family home. A climbing vine twines round the pergola, where the guests sit and savour the delights of country

cooking. If you warm to Latin charm, give your order to the Brylcreemed waiter.

### El Asador de Aranda★★

Avinguda del Tibidabo, 31
☎ 93 417 01 15
Avinguda Tibidabo rail stn.
Closed Sun. eve.

You come here for the decor – the Moorish entrance to this *Modernista* house is like a harem. In summer, on the terrace, they invariably serve shoulder of lamb grilled in an old-fashioned charcoal oven. Before leaving, climb the tower for the unique view.

### La Balsa★★

Infanta Isabel, 4
☎ 93 211 50 48
Avinguda Tibidabo rail stn.
Closed Sun. and Mon. lunch.

A restaurant nestling on the Tibidabo hillside, with a straw awning that blends in with

the greenery. Designed by Tusquets, It won a prize in 1979. With comfortable sofas and a choice of books, it is delightfully relaxing.The hake tartare and red-fruit sorbet are as light as air.

### Atlantic Restaurant★★

Avinguda del Tibidabo, 50
☎ 93 418 52 04
Open Mon.-Sat.

The first of the Atlantic's two main advantages is its marvellous view over the

Mediterranean. Add to this a menu full of sophisticated flavours and you won't regret having come this far. There are mussels stuffed with liver, rice with clams, sole stuffed with prawns in oyster sauce, and *magret de canard* with raspberries (5,000-7,000 ptas).

## La Venta★★
**Plaça del Doctor Andreu,**
**☎ 93 212 64 55**
**Closed Sun. Take a taxi.**

This pastel-coloured open-air café perched on top of the Tibidabo still has a late 19th-century air and old-fashioned charm. It's the ideal place for couples, who can huddle up to the stove in winter or dream on the terrace in summer while sharing a *mató de panses amb melles*, a sweet made from honey and currants .

## Bonanova★
**Sant Gervasi de Cassoles, 103**
**☎ 93 417 10 33**
**Plaça J. Folguera rail stn**
**Closed Sun. eve. and Mon.**

This family restaurant is reminiscent of a 1900's gaming room. The *Modernista* decor

of coloured *azulejos*, black and white tiled floor and tarnished mirrors hasn't aged a bit. From rabbit and snails to tasty fried fish, the menu wavers between land and sea. Worth getting out the map for!

## Ribera

## Cal Pep★★
**Plaça de les Olles, 8**
**☎ 93 319 61 83**
**Metro Jaume I**
**Closed Sun. and Mon. lunch.**

At Ribera you have to stand at the *barra* (bar) to try out the chef's various suggestions. He concocts fried food and dishes of the day – *supions* and *tellines*, *pulpitos* and shellfish – right before your eyes. A slice of life to savour!

## El Raïm★
**Pescateria, 6**
**☎ 93 319 20 98**
**Metro Jaume I**
**Closed Sat. and Sun.**

A small, unspoilt inn. One of the oldest and most popular locations in the city, run by an equally authentic and colourful owner. Amadeu runs a tight ship, single-handedly navigating between monkfish soup, *sopa*

*de rape*, and homemade stew, *guisos caseros*.

## Future★★
**Carrer Fusina, 5**
**☎ 93 319 92 99**
**Mon.-Sat. 8.30am-11pm.**

This loft, with its rather severe decor of white bricks and aluminium bar, is the latest place to see and be seen. Try the bar menu – we recommend the vegetable lasagne in a tomato and goat's cheese sauce. If you're planning a round of the bars in Plaça Del Born, currently the in-district, it's the ideal place to start. Make sure you don't miss out!

## Eixample

## Semproniana★★
**Rosellò, 148**
**☎ 93 453 18 20**
**Metro Diagonal.**

Creative cuisine based on local produce – crab and salmon mille feuilles, black sausage lasagne, and pig's trotter and pine nut terrine. The cosy, candlelit setting and old furniture will make you want to stay. Very good value for money (lunch menu 1,500 ptas).

## Casa Calvet★★★
**Casp, 48**
**☎ 93 412 40 12**
**Metro Urquinaona**
**Closed Sun.**

Set in one of the houses built by Gaudí (see p. 28), which used to house a textile business, Casa Calvet resembles a loft with wooden beams and traditionally stuccoed walls. Among the chef's recommendations are tasty cockle salad, delicious fresh lasagne with scampi, melting fillet of sole with cava, and mouth-watering white chocolate mousse.

## Madrid-Barcelona★★★

**Aragò, 282**
☎ 93 215 70 26
**Metro Passeig de Gràcia**
**Closed Sat., Sun. and public holidays.**

Not very far from the Tàpies foundation, this former railway station has been converted into a *tapas* bar serving omelettes, squid and aubergines (eggplants) – with a slice of nostalgia thrown in.

## Cal Boter★

**Tordera, 62**
☎ 93 458 84 62
**Metro Diagonal**
**Closed Mon.**

A good opportunity to explore the former village of Gràcia and the district's honest cuisine. Bistrot tables, *azulejos*, old-fashioned portraits and a blackboard displaying the dish of the day set the tone. The menu includes omelette with wild asparagus and prawns, peppers stuffed with cod, and pigs' trotters with snails. Set meal 950 ptas.

### Raval

## Casa Leopoldo★★★

**San Rafael, 24**
☎ 93 441 30 14
**Closed Sun. eve. and Mon.**
**Metro Liceu.**

In dining rooms decorated with yellow and blue *azulejos*, you'll be served the best *pà amb tomaquet* (see p. 10) in the city, as well as fried young fish, prawns and scampi. The customary presence of the famous writers Vázquez Montalbán, Marsé, and Mendoza may explain the dubious relation between cost and quality. Perhaps it's the price of fame.

### Ramblas

## Egipte★

**La Rambla, 79**
☎ 93 317 95 45
**Metro Liceu**
**Open every day.**

A good place to come if you're trying to make ends meet (set lunch around 985 ptas), where intellectuals, students, shopkeepers and architects from the Boqueria mingle. A friendly atmosphere in a rustic setting that matches the simple menu of cold ham, sausages and *matò*, fromage frais.

## Les Quinze Nits★

**Plaça Reial, 6**
☎ 93 317 30 75
**Metro Drassanes**
**Open every day.**

Quality, price and location all come together under the arches of the Plaça Reial.

Don't pass on the 995 ptas menu – it's currently one of the best deals around. Great value for money.

### Diagonal

## Rancho Grande★★

**Avinguda Diagonal, 73**
☎ 93 307 07 05
**Metro Selva de Mar**
**Open Mon.-Sat. lunchtime.**

A restaurant off the beaten track, with no sign up outside – it's for connoisseurs only. Rancho Grande has the air of a village inn and lunch is whatever's simmering in the pot – fresh produce in season, grilled snails or leeks, *calçots* or prawns, with *ensaimadas*, Majorcan pastries, to complete the menu. When the owner is happy with the tip, she rings the bell.

### Sitges

## Maricel★★

**Passeig de la Ribera, 6**
☎ 93 894 20 54.

On the *paseo* (promenade) facing the bay, the terrace between sea and sky (*mar i cel*) hence Maricel, serves classic Mediterranean cuisine – *paella marinera*, with fresh fish, *escalivada*, sweet peppers, aubergines (eggplants), and onions marinated in olive oil. Is your Catalan up to ordering from the menu?

# DAYTIME CAFÉS AND TEAROOMS

## Ciutadella

### Hivernacle Café

Parc de la Ciutadella
Passeig Picasso
☎ 93 310 22 91
Metro Ciutadella
Mon.-Sat. 10am-midnight,
Sun. 10am-5pm.

A greenhouse dating from the Great Exhibition of 1888 has become the most romantic summer garden café, with luxuriant plants,

purring cats and even a melodious fountain which echoes the live jazz which is played there on Wednesdays.

## Ramblas

### Bar Jardin

Portaferissa, 17
Metro Liceu

Take me to the Casbah! A camel and oasis create an exotic atmosphere. There are also little garden tables and pop-art sofas which all add up to an interesting mix of styles and a haven for the young.

## Raval

### Granja Viader

Xuclà, 4
☎ 93 318 34 86
Metro Catalunya
Closed Sun. and Mon. morn.

*Granja* has found the formula for a tearoom to please all ages, from children to little old ladies, and from creative types to people laden with shopping bags. Here's where you'll find the best crème brûlée, Swiss chocolate with whipped cream and homemade lemon madeleines in the city.

### Café que pone 'meubles Navarro'

Riera Alta, 4/6
☎ 907 18 90 96
Tue.-Sat. 11am-midnight,
Sun. 5pm-midnight.

Come here to drink a *copa* on a comfortable sofa or colonial chaise longue, or enjoy a tasty *bocadillo* or slice of homemade cheesecake in an informal setting. Exhibitions of photos and paintings cover the walls of this friendly Raval café. It's a place to relax and unwind in.

## Horchateria Sirvent

Parlament, 56
☎ 93 441 27 20
Metro Sant Antoni
Open every day.

Slake your thirst near the Ronda San Pau with *borchata*, barley water, or a *turròn*-flavoured ice cream (see page 111). People traditionally hesitate between *granizada*, coffee-flavoured, crushed ice, and a delicious ice-cream cornet. You can worry about your diet tomorrow!

## Barrio Gòtico

### Bon Mercat

Bajada Llibreteria, 1
☎ 93 315 29 08
Metro Jaume I.
Closed Sun.

For 95 ptas, you can savour a strong black coffee, or *tallat* with a dash of milk, with the heady aroma of Guatemalan coffee, Ethiopian mocca or *gran altura mezcla*. Drink it standing at the crowded bar with a tasty *bocadillo*.

### La Pineda

Carrer del Pi, 16
☎ 93 302 43 93
Metro Liceu
Mon.-Sat.
9am-3pm, 5-10pm,
Sun. 11am-3pm,
7-10pm.

A small stall where you can stand and eat *tapas* at the marble counter or imitate the real thing by sitting on barrels. Escale anchovies, Serrano and Aragon hams and *chorizo iberico*, spiced sausage. If you like the owner's wares, you can buy some more on credit!

## Bar del Pi

**Plaça Sant Josep Oriol, 1**
**☎ 93 302 21 23**
**Metro Liceu**
**Open every day.**

The Plaça del Pi is without doubt the most pleasant and charming terrace in the city. Intellectuals, the 'divine left', and artists short of inspiration come here. Newspapers are available for customers to read and the coffee percolator makes a change from the sounds of jazz in the square.

## El Café d'Estiu

**Plaça Sant Iu, 5**
**Metro Jaume I.**

In summer, a few tables are set up near a refreshing pool in the courtyard of the F. Marès museum, right in the heart of the Barrio Gòtico. Large white parasols and a wooden stall offer busy visitors a delicious break in a quiet haven.

## Laie

**Pau Claris, 85**
**☎ 93 318 17 39**
**Metro Urquinaona**
**Mon.-Sat. 10am-9pm.**

For a literary and gourmet break, this tea-room-bookshop is a dream come true. Magazines from all over the world, art books and philosophical treatises mingle with home-made pastries and the smell of coffee. A perfect blend of nourishment for body and soul.

## Mauri

**Rambla de Catalunya, 103**
**☎ 93 215 09 98**
**Metro Diagonal.**

Smart young mothers with babies and well-dressed ladies come here to indulge their sweet tooth. A confectioners and cake shop where perfect taste, elaborate display shelves and black and gold window displays are the order of the day.

### Sitges

## Villa Lola

**Passeig de la Ribera.**

Beneath the pearly façade of a *Modernista* villa, the terrace of this bar serves delicious *zumos naturales*, natural fruit juices, and South Seas cocktails. Good jazz adds to the atmosphere as you gaze out to sea.

## La Estrella Sitges

**Carrer Major, 52**
**☎ 93 894 00 79**
**Closed Mon.**

This patisserie is decorated from floor to ceiling with frescoes,

bottles of liqueur and boxes of sweets. All the traditional treats await you in the *salò de té* – why not try a little glass of Sitges malmsey, the local liqueur, too?

### Ribera

## El Xampanyet

**Montcada, 22**
**☎ 93 319 70 03**
**Metro Jaume I**
**Tue.-Sun. noon-4pm, 6.30-11.30pm.**

A small, friendly inn run by the same family since 1929 Colourful *azulejos*, flasks hanging from the ceiling and wine barrels set the tone. Try tasty anchovies, olives, and marinated fish with Penedès white wine.

**A**    **B**

Traversera   de   les   Corts

PL. DR. I. BARRAQUER

PLAÇA FRANCESC MACIÀ

Av. de Sarrià

Galileo

Numància

C. Buenos Ai

Av.

C. de Brasil

de   Madrid

de

Carrer del Marquès de Sentmenat

d'Entença

Tarradellas

d'Urgell

PL. DEL CENTRE

Carrer

de   Berlin

Josep

Carrer

Vilodomat

de

**1**

Carrer

de

de

Rocafort

Calàbria

de

Carrer

PLAÇA JOAN PEIRÓ

**RENFE Central Sants**

C. St Antoni

PLAÇA DELS PAÏSOS CATALANS

Carrer

Borrell

Comte

Carrer

de

la

Creu

*Parc de l'Espanya Industrial*

Carrer   de   Tarragona

Carrer

d'Entença

Carrer

de

d'Aragó

C. de Gavà

Carrer del Moianès

Coberta

C. de la Bordeta

*Parc Joan Miró*

Carrer

de

Comte

del

de

Carrer

Plaça de Toros Les Arenes

Avinguda   Granvia

PLAÇA D'ESPANYA

Grand   Via

Sepúlveda

**2**

Av. del Marquès de Comillas

**Palau de la Metalúrgia**

Av. de la Reina M. Cristina

PLAÇA DE L'UNIVERS

Avinguda

Carrer

**SANT ANTONI**

Floridablanca

Carrer

de

**Palau de Congressos**

Av. de Rius i Taulet

de   Mistral

Tamarit

**Poble Espanyol**

**Palau del Cinquantenari**

C.

de

**Mercat de Sant Antoni**

Avinguda

de

**Palau de Victòria Eugènia**

**Palaus Alfons XIII**

**Palau Municipal d'Esports**

Carrer

de   Sant   Pau

**Palau Nacional**

**Museu d'Art de Catalunya**

**Museu Etnològic**

Ronda

del

**MUNTANYA**

l'Estadi

**Museu Archeològic**

**Palau Sant Jordi**

**Palau Albéniz**

**Fondació Joan Miró**

**Sant P del Car**

**DE**   MONTJUÏC

Nou

**MONTJUÏC**

Avinguda   de

Carrer

**3**

C.

del

Mordals

de

*Miramar*

**Castell de Montjuïc**

Carretera   de   Miramar

Passeig   de   Jos

| 0 | 200 | 400 | 600 m |
| 0 | 200 | 400 | 600 yds |

**A**    **B**

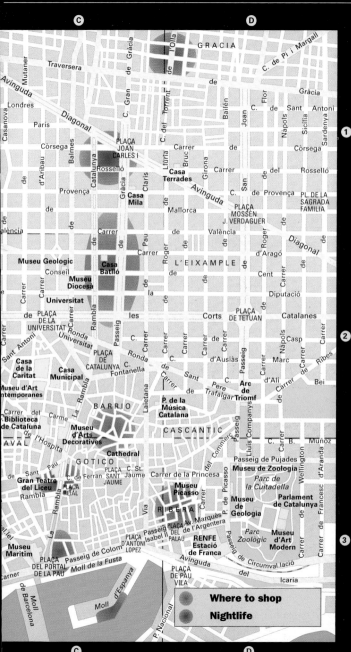

# Shopping Practicalities

The people of Barcelona have a nose for business – hardly surprising since the city was founded on commerce, and trading has taken place here for 2,000 years – so no need to worry, there are shops on every street corner.

The most stylish shops (selling jewellery, designer labels and luxury clothes) are on the Passeig de Gràcia, Rambla de Catalunya and in the area around the Turò park. Arts and crafts and small businesses liven up the old quarters (Barrio Gotico and Ribera), the Boqueria market on the Ramblas opens very early in the morning and the port attracts many shoppers too with the new Maremagnum

## FINDING YOUR WAY

Next to each address in the Shopping and Nightlife sections we have given its location on the map of Barcelona on pages 80–81.

centre, which is also open on Sundays.

## SHOP OPENING HOURS

Most shops open Monday to Saturday, 10am to 2pm and 4.30 to 8pm, with food shops opening an hour earlier in the morning. Make a note of the opening hours if you don't want to get caught out – all the shops close for lunch, with the exception of the big shopping centres, Illà on the Diagonal and Corte Inglès in the Plaça de Catalunya, which stay open all day long. Some shops close on Saturday afternoons, but the Maremagnum shopping centre located in the port is open from 11am to 11pm.

## PAYING FOR YOUR PURCHASES

Most shopkeepers accept credit cards (American Express, Mastercard and Visa International) and, of course, cash. You just present your card and sign the till receipt in the usual way. In the event of loss or theft, call the relevant centre in Madrid:

**American Express**
☎ 91 572 03 03
**Diners**
☎ 91 547 40 00
or Barcelona:
**Mastercard**
☎ 93 315 25 12
**Visa**
☎ 93 315 25 12.

Traveller's cheques are commonly accepted. You can also pay with Eurocheques in some establisments.

## SALES

The majority of shops hold their sales from the second week in January to the end of February and in July and August. They're not as spectacular as the London sales but you can usually find reductions of anything from 25 to 50%, except at Zara (clothes), where the prices are really slashed.

Prices are displayed everywhere and it isn't done to bargain, apart from in flea-markets where you'll find that the Catalans are tough negotiators and every penny counts. So, be firm, forewarned is forearmed! You can apply for a visitor's shopping card from:

### Turisme de Barcelona:
Plaça de Catalunya, 17-5
☎ 93 304 32 32
🅕 93 304 33 26.

This card provides certain benefits (including discounts of around 10%) in more than 200 shops where the sign *'Barcelona, ciutat de compres'* ('Barcelona, the shoppers' paradise') is displayed in the window.

Worth getting if you're planning to do a lot of shopping!

### CUSTOMS DUTY ON PURCHASES

If you're a citizen of a member state of the European Union, you won't have to pay any customs duty on your purchases, whatever their value, but you will have to show the receipts. Non EU-citizens are exempt from paying VAT on purchases with a value of more than 15,000 ptas. Remember to ask for a *'Tax-free cheque'* when making your purchase. On leaving Spain, make sure you have the 'cheques' stamped at customs so that you can cash them at a branch of the Banco exterior de España when you arrive home. If you buy a work of art or antique declared as *de valor patrimonial* ('of national value'), you must request an export licence from the Spanish equivalent of the National Heritage. The vendor will help you with this process. You can insist on a certificate of authenticity. An invoice is always essential – you can be asked for it at customs and it will be useful to you if you want to sell your purchase at a later date, or if you're burgled and need to fill in a claim form for your insurance company. Be on the lookout for forgeries and stolen goods.

### TRANSPORT FACILITIES

If you buy a piece of furniture or bulky object, there's no problem about having it delivered home. Simply give the delivery company a photocopy of your invoice, and they'll make out the delivery note.

**UPS**, United Parcel Service freephone
☎ 900 10 24 10.
This haulier makes deliveries worldwide and can arrange immediate dispatch if required.

**SEUR** ☎ 93 571 72 73.
This company takes on packages of all sizes and provides a free estimate for your consignments

**GEFCO** ☎ 93 843 73 14.
This large national and international haulage firm will guarantee you professional and urgent delivery if necessary.

If you export one of the latter, you could be prosecuted for possession of stolen goods. Buy only from established traders and be wary of anything that looks like a real bargain.

**Customs:**
Passeig Josep Carner 27,
☎ 93 443 30 08.

# WOMEN'S FASHION: READY-TO-WEAR, ACCESSORIES, SHOES AND DESIGNER CLOTHES

You may dream of being a *Barefoot Contessa,* or stealing the show in *High Society.* You may aspire to taking *Breakfast at Tiffany's,* whilst in search of *La Dolce Vita,* but if you find yourself attending *Four Weddings and a Funeral* you will certainly need some *Pret-à-Porter.* Cinematic fantasies apart, if you'd like to inject a little Spanish style into your wardrobe, here are some places to try.

### Forum

C. Ferlandina, 31 (C2)
☎ 93 441 80 18
Tue.-Sat.
10.30am-2pm,
5-8.30pm

Just a step away from the Museum of Contemporary Art, the work of sixty jewellery designers is on display in this workshop/ gallery, and shop run by a young German woman. The pieces are made in limited editions and prices range from 4,000 to 100,000 ptas. Make sure you come here if you like unique contemporary jewellery and don't forget to take a look at the workshop to see how it is made.

### Muxart

Rosellón 230 (C/D1)
☎ 93 488 10 64
Mon.-Sat.
10am-2pm, 4.30-8.30pm.

Muxart is an outstanding Catalan designer who excels in the art of making boots and ankle boots, both with and without laces. Made in Minorca, they're distinctive for the detail of the finish and the quality of the materials. Come here if you're looking for originality and expect to pay 20,000-23,000 ptas.

### Loewe

Paseo de Gràcia, 35 (C1/2)
☎ 93 216 04 00
Metro Paseo de Gràcia
Mon.-Sat. 9.30am-2pm, 4.30-8pm.

Loewe uses the elegant façade of the Casa Lléo Morera as a setting for its luxury leather goods. Like its first cousins Gucci and Hermès,

it supplies top of the range goods. With its 150-year tradition of quality and luxury, the company has all the know-how needed to produce perfect leather articles and colourful, elegant silk scarves.

## Groc

**Muntaner, 385 ((C1/2)**
☎ 93 202 30 77
**Mon.-Sat. 10am-2pm,
4.30-8pm.**

One of the first places to have sold clothes by designers such as Antonio Miró, for both men and women. Groc has added its own label to these and offers a choice of sophisticated, elegant garments made of cotton, linen and silk in fluid simple shapes and designs.

## Casa Oliveras

**Dagueria, 11 (not on map)**
☎ 93 315 19 05
**Metro Jaume I
Mon.-Fri. 9am-1pm,
4-7pm.**

Who says Catalan embroidery has gone out of style? Behind the cathedral, in a shop with unusual porcelain lampshades, Rosa embroiders decorative detail that will give ordinary dresses a slightly antique look.

## El Mercadillo

**Portaferissa, 17 (C2)**
☎ 93 317 85 64
**Metro Catalunya
Mon.-Sat. 10.30am-8pm.**

With a cardboard camel and New Age music to greet you, you'll know you're in an unusual place. The owner sells a combination of streetwear, casual wear and secondhand clothes, including the cool look for psychedelic evenings – platform shoes, fluorescent skirts, ponchos and shirts made of African fabrics – to suit those who like to be a little different.

## Casa Ciutad

**Avinguda Portal de l'Angel, 14 (C2)**
☎ 93 317 04 33
**Mon.-Fri. 10am-8.30pm,
Sat. 10am-9pm.**

Since 1892, the company has supplied *articulos de tocador* (toiletry articles), including a formidable array of brushes and combs, some of them Spanish-style, to hold complicated hairdos in place (3,500-14,000 ptas).

## LA MANUAL ALPARGATERA

**Carrer Avinyào, 7**
☎ 93 301 01 72
**Metro Liceu
Mon.-Sat. 9.30am-1.30pm,
4.30-8pm.**

Behind a whitewashed façade lie espadrilles of every different shape and size – boot-style, with laces or embroidery, coloured and striped. The workshop is on the premises and you can order a made-to-measure pair from the owner, who supplies the likes of Jack Nicholson and Pope John Paul II. Or why not buy some mini-espadrilles for the new baby (500 to 6,000 ptas)?

## Lydia Delgado

**Minerva, 21 (C1)**
☎ 93 415 99 98
**Metro Diagonal
Mon.-Sat. 10am-2pm,
5-8.30pm.**

This young Spanish designer shows her chic, sexy clothes in

a fifties setting, with suits priced at around 75,000 ptas and avant-garde short skirts selling for 45,000 ptas, as well as sixties Cubist dresses and hipster trousers – all up-to-date styles as dynamic as their designer

## Julie Sohn

**Consell de Cent, 308 (D2)**
**☎ 93 487 84 24**
**Mon.-Sat. 10.30am-8.30pm.**

Julie Sohn is a young Korean designer who creates demure styles more reminiscent of Jil Sander than Jean-Paul Gaultier. Made in Barcelona, the raw wool suits and poplin shirts create a no-frills, trendy traditional look (a suit costs 60,000-70 000 ptas).

## Josep Font
## Luz Diaz

**Paseo de Gràcia, 106 (C1/2)**
**☎ 93 415 65 50**
**Metro Diagonal**
**Every day 10am-8pm.**

Long, pure, fluid lines and earth shades, brown and black add a touch of sophistication to the collections of these two Catalan designers. Elegant women who like pared-down designs will find

plain clothes enhanced with beautiful patterns in the weave, or simple, discreet accessories.

## Joieria Sunyer

**Gran via de les Corts**
**Catalanes, 660**
**☎ 93 317 22 93**
**Metro Urquinaona**
**Mon.-Fri.**
**10am-1.30pm, 4.30-8pm.**

Since 1835, five generations of jewellers have succeeded one another in this Art Deco setting opposite the Ritz, a magnificent showcase for gilded silver bracelets (60,000 ptas) and jewellery in exclusive designs passed down from father to son. A custom jewellers providing an old-fashioned service.

## Replay

**Paseo de Gràcia, 60 (C1/2)**
**Mon.-Sat. 10am-9pm**

Replay is shop-café-restaurant. Take a look at the Replay basic Italian collection displayed in a very attractive setting of pale wooden floors and parchment lampshades. After you've done

your shopping, have a coffee in one of the city's most beautiful *Modernista* market halls – the ideal pick-me-up for shop-weary husbands!

## Jean Pierre Bua

**Diagonal, 469 (C/D1)**
**☎ 93 439 71 00**
**Metro Diagonal**
**Mon.-Sat.**
**10am-2pm, 4.30-8.30pm .**

With sexy layering, sophisticated recycling, scandalous see-throughs, chic or ethnic, classic, retro or modern styles, designers from Sybilla,

Jean-Paul Gaultier and Marcel Marougiu to Jean Colonna, Yamamoto and Vivienne Westwood are here to give you an unusual and glamorous new look.

## Zara

**Avinguda Portal de l'Angel, 24**
☎ 93 301 29 25
**Metro Catalunya**
**Avinguda Diagonal, 584**
☎ 93 414 29 46
**Metro Diagonal**
**Pelai, 58**
☎ 93 301 09 78
**Metro Catalunya**
**Rambla de Catalunya, 67**
☎ 93 487 08 18
**Metro Passeig de Gràcia**
**Mon.-Sat. 10am-8pm.**

Zara is the latest brand of Spanish clothes. Its men's, women's and children's lines are inexpensive versions of the latest looks in good quality fabrics. In a pale wood setting, and with styles ranging from basic to trendy, there are sweaters from about 4,900 ptas and summer suits for 16,000 ptas.

## Divine

**Ramelleres, 24 (C2)**
☎ 93 412 61 70
**Metro Catalunya.**
**Mon.-Sat.**
**11am-9pm**

### LOVE AT FIRST SIGHT

## LA PLUMISTA

**Banys Nous, 13 (C3)**
☎ 93 305 52 94
**Metro Liceu**
**5.30-8pm.**

This shop, which is one of a kind, is a real find. Curious visitors, struck at first by the smell of mothballs, will wonder what's in the faded cardboard boxes lining the walls from floor to ceiling. They in fact contain secondhand feathers, as the owner of the shop was in her heyday when elegant women wore hats and gloves to go to the Liceu theatre. *La Plumista* proudly displays her *lloronas*, 'weeping' ostrich feathers in iridescent colours priced at 7,000 ptas each. Don't miss this shop with its old world charm.

Barcelona's wildest fashion victims buy their clothes in this pink setting beneath Warhol's Marilyn Monroe. Creations from young Spanish designers include cycling shorts, metallic blouson jackets and fluorescent micro T-shirts by Juanito, Vacas Flacas, Albarran and other underground names.

## Lailo

**Riera Baixa, 20**
☎ 93 441 37 49
**Metro Liceu**
**Mon.-Thu. 5.30-9pm**
**Fri.-Sat. 10am-2pm,**
**5.30-9pm.**

This exhibition space, school and workshop outlet, all rolled into one, lies just a stone's throw from the Museum of Contemporary Art. Jordi Vizcaino runs a good-quality secondhand clothes department with shawls, Audrey Hepburn-style dresses, silk capes and top hats (11,000 ptas). Jordi also holds *tertulies* here, lively meetings at which poetry and music are discussed. A new version of the Bohemian lifestyle in an unusual, appealing setting.

# MEN'S FASHION

Men's fashion comes in every possible shape and form. Whatever style you go for – formal or casual, classic or trendy, intellectual or sporty, Latin lover or cool dude – you'll find clothes to suit you in this selection of shops.

measure winter clothes for you. Natural fibres (cotton, linen and wool) create supple comfortable garments. Place an order at the start of your stay and you can take it away with you when you leave.

## El Transwaal
Hospital, 67 (C3)
☎ 93 301 91 18
Metro Liceu
Mon.-Sat. morning
9.30am-1.30pm, 4.30-8pm.

A shop that's worth the visit for the sign alone. A shop-window dummy in a starched hat welcomes you to a world of

## Adolfo Dominguez
Passeig de Gràcia, 32 (C1/2)
☎ 93 487 41 70
Passeig de Gràcia, 89 (C1/2)
☎ 93 215 13 39
Diagonal, 490 (C/D1)
☎ 93 416 11 92
Mon.-Sat. 10am-2pm,
4.30-8pm.

If you're planning a business meeting or romantic dinner with the woman in your life, the collections of this internationally-famous designer are absolutely not to be missed. High-quality fabrics and natural colours give Dominguez' refined clothes a sober elegance.

## Otman Chentouf
Carrer Banys Vells, 21a (C3)
☎ 93 441 22 26
Mon.-Sat. 11am-2pm,
4-9pm.

Banys Vells street, in the Born district, is where artisan designers are once again to be found working at looms and painting on silk. There is also a Moroccan tailor who will make made-to-

professional uniforms, including a waiter's dinner suit and chef's outfit. Ideal for impressing the guests at your next dinner party.

## Camper

**Centre commercial el Triangle, Pelaio 13-37 (C2)**
☎ 933 024 924
**Mon.-Sat.
10.30am-10pm.**

In the newly-built shopping centre in the Plaça de Catalunya, you'll get off on the right foot with Camper's crepe soles and colourful supple leathers. Innovative shoe designs for everyone.

## Planeta X

**Boters (C2)**
☎ 93 301 34 80
**Mon.-Sat. 10am-8.30pm.**

A trendy address for fans of streetwear, techno and the like, not far from the cathedral. You can choose from a selection of all-purpose, all-terrain outfits (the high tech Cocoa line got our vote) and set off to take the city by storm.

## Gonzalo Comella

**Diagonal, 478 (C/D1)**
☎ 93 416 15 16
**Metro Diagonal
Mon.-Sat. 10am-2pm,
4.30-8.30pm**
**Passeig de Gràcia, 6 (C1/2)**
☎ 93 412 66 00
**Metro Catalunya
Mon.-Sat. 10am-8pm.**

You'll find fashionable clothes for both town and country, including parkas by A. Miró, Ralph Lauren pullovers, Hugo Boss suits, Armani shirts and Church's shoes.

## Ovlas Men

**Portaferissa, 25, Tienda 34 (C2)**
☎ 93 412 52 29
**Metro Liceu
Every day 10am-2pm,
4.30-8.30pm.**

Drainpipe or hipster trousers, close-fitting jackets and Mao shirts – sixties-style menswear for those who don't want to wear Levi's. With trousers from stretch material, sexy shirts and toreador-style jackets, you are bound to cut a quite considerable dash on the dance floor.

## Sombreria Obach

**Call, 2 (C3)**
☎ 93 318 40 94
**Metro Liceu
Mon.-Sat.
10am-1.30pm, 4-8pm.**

In the heart of the old town, Sombreria Obach have been making hats for three generations.
Take your pick from caps (1,000-4,000 ptas), Basque berets (*boinas*, 2,000 ptas), *barretina catalana* (Catalan caps) to wear pulled over one ear

## UMBRELLAS FOR ALL

### JULIO GOMEZ

**La Rambla, 104**
☎ 93 412 72 58
**Metro Liceu
Mon.-Sat. 9am-1.30pm,
4-8pm.**

This is one of the oldest businesses on the Rambla. Since 1865, the people of Barcelona having been coming here to have umbrella ribs and walking-sticks repaired. Buy a *baston* (walking stick)(400-12,000 ptas) and make a grand entrance at the Liceu theatre. The stars of musical comedies and Gene Kelly placed orders here. Why not you?

(900 ptas), and light straw panamas (6,000-11,000 ptas) for the look that suits you best.

# CHILDREN'S CLOTHES AND GAMES

In a country with one of the lowest birth rates in Europe it isn't surprising that children are treated like royalty. Like the Italians, the Spanish have always loved children and you will find that they are readily accepted in most places. Here are some suggestions for places to spoil your own.

### El Rey de la Magia

**Princessa, 11 (D3)**
☎ 93 319 73 93
**Metro Jaume 1**
**Mon.-Sat. morn.**
**10am-2pm, 5-8pm.**

Everything for children who want to be magicians when they grow up. Jokes and tricks of every kind, including conjuring tricks and sleight-of-hand, that are just the thing for the budding magician. With a blood-red shop-window display and a sign in the form of a turbaned genie with a hypnotic stare, be prepared to fall under its spell.

### Juguetes Foyé

**Banys Nous, 13 (C3)**
☎ 93 302 03 89
**Metro Liceu**
**Mon.-Sat. 10am-2pm,**
**4.30-8pm.**

The oldest toy shop in the city; four generations of the Foyé family have already kept the children of Barcelona happy. There are metal toys for collectors and wooden horses in papier mâché (12,000 ptas), musical boxes (14,000 ptas), steam engines and fancy dress.

### Drap

**Pi, 14 (C3)**
☎ 93 318 14 87
**Metro Liceu**
**Mon.-Sat. 10am-1.30pm,**
**4.30-8.30pm.**

Few little girls will be able to resist these delightful doll's houses. Palaces, chalets and two-storey Victorian houses cost 40,000-400,000 ptas. Don't forget that once the dream house has been chosen, its walls still have to be papered, fire-places have to be fitted, curtains hung and finally it has to be furnished.

### Rosès

**Avinguda Portal de l'Angel, 15 (C2)**
☎ 93 302 03 34
**Metro Catalunya**
**Mon.-Sat. morn.**
**10am-1.30pm, 4.30-8pm.**

In a street where an angel is supposed to have appeared, it isn't surprising to find a shop selling *figuras para belenes* (figures for the crib). The traditional cribs of Murcia and Olot (6000 ptas) always include a fertility symbol, the *caganer*, as explained on page 14.

## Kiddy's Class

**Avinguda Porta de l'Angel, 16**
☎ 93 301 15 27
**Metro Catalunya**
**Mon.-Sat. 10am-8.30pm.**

A great choice of clothes at unbeatable prices. Good value sportswear with a hint of the traditional and a touch of the classroom. Shirts 2,700 ptas, T-shirts 1,500 ptas and dresses 4,000 ptas.

## Sardina Submarina

**Cardenal Casañas, 1 (C3)**
☎ 933 171 179
**Mon.-Sat. 9.30am-2pm, 4.30-8.30pm**

This colourful shop behind the Ramblas sells mainly wooden toys – scooters, cookery and tea sets, puppets and Danish mobiles, as well as board games and pretty lamps for all ages.

shirts, Sioux-Indian sweaters, and exclusive bikinis and swimsuits, though prices are quite high.

## Imaginarium

**Marina Village, 11 or Rambla de Cataluna, 31 or Maremagnum L40 (C1/2)**
☎ 93 487 67 54
**Mon.-Sat. 10am-8.30pm.**

A colourful and brightly-lit setting for open-air games – trampolines, slides, swings and inflatable swimming pools. And if you can't really see where you'll put it all, fall back on the skittles, rocking horses, spinning-tops, drums and other smaller toys.

## Oilily

**Tenor Vinas, 1 (B1)**
☎ 93 201 84 79
**Ferrocarril Muntaner**
**Mon.-Sat. 10.15am-2pm, 4.30-8.15pm.**

A riot of colour and pretty prints will add a cheerful note to your children's wardrobes, with little floral skirts, checked lumberjack

## Menkes

**Gran via de les Corts Catalanes, 646 (A/D2)**
☎ 93 318 86 47
**Metro Passeig de Gràcia**
**Mon.-Sat. 9.30am-1.30pm, 4.30-8pm.**

Founded in 1950, Menkes is the place to go for fancy dress costumes, e.g. Sleeping Beauty, toreador and

## El Ingenio

**Rauric, 6,**
☎ 93 317 71 38.
**Metro Liceu**
**Mon.-Sat. 10am-1.30pm, 4.15-8pm.**

A shop with a carnival atmosphere. Since 1838, the Cardona family have been making masks and *cap-grossos*, the giants' heads that parade through the streets of Barcelona and Sitges. You can see a workshop at the back of the shop where the unfinished papier-mâché heads have something very bizarre and surreal about them. Even Dali was fascinated by this highly unusual place.

flamenco dancer – with or without false eyelashes (11,000 to 15,000 ptas). It's an incredible Aladdin's Cave, where children can find just the outfit they need to really make an impression at a fancy dress party back home.

# DEPARTMENT STORES AND SHOPPING ARCADES

Shops are usually open until around 7.30 or 8pm during the week and 6pm is a particularly busy time as people shop after work. However, don't forget that a few stores close for *siesta* after lunch (usually between 2 and 4.30pm), so don't expect all the shops to be open then. The most recent stores and arcades, Maremagnum and Illa, have striking window displays, a source of great pride to the people of Barcelona.

## El Corte Inglés

**Plaça de Catalunya, 14 (C2)**
**☎ 93 306 38 00**
**Metro Catalunya**
**Avinguda Diagonal, 617 (C/D1)**
**☎ 93 419 28 28**
**Metro Maria Cristina**
**Mon.-Sat. 10am-9.30pm.**

This famous department store stands in the Plaça de Catalunya like a vast Art Deco ocean liner. It is the city's biggest store and stocks a wide range of goods. However, be warned, prices are on the high side and the ladies' fashion department is a little on the staid side. Still, if you can't find anything you like, you can always enjoy the view from the restaurant.

## Maremagnum

**Moll d'Espanya (C3)**
**☎ 93 225 81 00**
**Metro Drassanes**
**Mon.-Sun. 11am-11pm.**

The most recent addition to the city's shore area and the pride of the people of Barcelona. This vast shopping centre has become an obligatory part of the Sunday stroll, with a mixture of cafés, restaurants, bars and shops. Maremagnum caters for all tastes, from the high-tech and kitsch to the eco-friendly and green. It's a bold construction of glass panels and wooden walkways.

## Boulevard Rosa

**Passeig de Gràcia, 55(C1/2)**
**☎ 93 215 83 31**
**Metro Plaça de Gràcia.**
**Avinguda Diagonal, 474 (C/D1)**
**☎ 93 215 83 31**
**Metro Diagonal**
**Mon.-Sat. 10.30am-8.30pm.**

Hoping to find strength in numbers, the first shopping centres flourished in Barcelona, as in London, in the seventies. There are over a hundred shops

## L'Illà

**Avinguda Diagonal, 557
(C/D1)
☎ 93 444 00 00
Metro Maria Cristina
Mon.-Sat. 10am-9pm.**

In the business district, on the Avinguda Diagonal, the three floors of this new shopping centre cater for the needs of the local office workers. You'll find many of the shops that are in Maremagnum (see left) are also here, plus Marks and Spencer and the Caprabo supermarket which sells food. It is extremely practical for the locals due to its strategic location and underground car park.

## NO NEED TO WORRY ABOUT THE DEMISE OF THE LOCAL SHOP!

Like all cities, Barcelona suffers from the 'shopping centre' syndrome, yet Spaniards have never been in favour of mass marketing. They still prefer their traditional markets, and the city has no less than forty-one covered markets. The community spirit and various commercial groups combine to produce a network of resistance across the city and small retailers courageously fend off attacks from the big boys.

at these Boulevard Rosa locations. The fashion, shoe, jewellery and perfume boutiques and stores, along with cafés and bars make them favourite meeting places on Friday nights for teenagers and young professionals. The selection of shops tends to be fairly trendy and includes Marcel's, the 'in' place to have a haircut in Barcelona (a cut costs 4,975 ptas at Diagonal).

## SPORTS GOODS AND GADGETS

The people of Barcelona take part in aquatic and mountain sports with equal enthusiasm. They're fanatical about football and balconies are decked with flags in the Barça colours during the football season. If you are particularly interested in sports goods and gadgets you will find plenty of choice here. In fact Barcelona had a very wide choice long before the Olympic Games came to town in 1992.

### La Botiga del Barça

**Maremagnum, local 27**
**Moll d'Espanya (C3)**
**☎ 93 225 80 45**
**Metro Barceloneta**
**Mon.-Sun. 11am-11pm.**

For ardent supporters of the local football team, you'll find football shirts, shorts, flags, caps, ash-trays and key rings in the Barça colours (red and blue). You can also visit the Camp Nou Stadium and museum (see p.19) for that total Barcelona football experience.

### Jonas

**Marina Village tenda, 15**
**Port Olímpic (C3)**
**☎ 93 225 15 68**
**Metro Barceloneta**
**Mon.-Fri. 10.30am-**
**12.30pm, 4-9.30pm,**
**Sat. 10.30am-9.30pm.**

A red-chrome Harley Davidson in the entrance sets the tone and you know this is a shop for real enthusiasts. Jonas specialises in extreme sports and you can get your snowboarding and surfing gear here, made of either fleece or light nylon –

so, choose waves or moguls according to your mood.

### Quera

**Petritxol, 2 (C2/3)**
**☎ 318 07 43**
**Metro Liceu**
**Mon.-Sat. 9.30am-1.30pm,**
**4.30-8pm.**

Leaf through a vast array of old maps and dusty tomes in this book-shop to discover interesting routes for your trekking expedition in the Pyrenees, or elsewhere. Familiar-ise yourself with rock climbing,

potholing, or more gentle
pursuits – the adventure starts
here.

## For Pilots

**Passeig de Gràcia, 55 (C1/2)
Tienda Avinguda Rosa, 18
☎ 93 215 96 35
Mon.-Sat. 10.30am-8.30pm.**

If you fancy yourself in a
magnificent leather flying jacket
this is the place to come. They
begin at around 38,000 ptas. You
can add a compass watch for
11,000 ptas and a flying belt for
3,500 ptas, not to mention
American aviator glasses.

## GADGETS
### Items d'Ho

**Mallorca, 251 (A2)
☎ 93 488 32 37
Mon.-Sat. 10am-8.30pm
Passeig de Gràcia, 55
Avinguda Rosa (C1/2)
☎ 93 216 09 41
Mon.-Sat. 10am-8.30pm.**

This shop specialises in gifts for
men. From key rings and luggage
to fashionable glasses cases and
chromium-plated watches,
everything has been carefully
designed and finished to please
your 'hombre'.

## Natura

**Maremagnum,
Moll d'Espanya (C3)
☎ 93 225 80 49
Metro Barceloneta
Mon-Sun. 11am-11pm
Consell de Cent, 304 (D2)
☎ 93 488 19 72
Mon.-Sat. 10am-8pm.**

For fans of environmentally-
friendly design, there are wood and
rattan lamps, Mexican mobiles
(490 ptas), candle holders, bird

cages, Afghan hats and T-shirts
defending the rights of the whale –
a little touch of Greenpeace – all
wrapped up in recycled paper.

## Dom

**Passeig de Gràcia, 76 (C1/2)
☎ 93 487 11 81
Metro Passeig de Gràcia
Petritxol, 14 (C2/3)
☎ 93 318 56 23
Mon.-Sat. 10am-2pm, 4-8pm.**

Wacky and unusual
designs, bags made from brightly
coloured nylon, pens in the form
of flowers. Humorous gadgets
galore in this amusing shop.

## D Barcelona

**Diagonal, 367 (C/D1)
☎ 93 216 03 46
Metro Passeig de Gràcia
Mon.-Sat.10.30am-2pm,
4.30-9.30pm.
Maremagnum, local 39 (C3)
☎ 93 225 80 86
Mon.-Sat. 11am-10pm.**

### COLONEL TAPIOCA
**Marià Cubi, 174, ☎ 93 202
22 25. Mon. afternoon-Sat.
10.30am-2pm, 4.30-8.15pm
Ferrocarril Sant Gervasi.**

The *Raiders of the Lost Ark*
must have got their gear here.
If you fancy going on a safari,
camel expedition, jeep rally, or just
like the 'Out of Africa' look, come
along to the Colonel's and he'll
supply you with everything you
need. From the penknife to the
survival kit, by way of the portable
solar stove, you won't be short of
anything next time you leave.
*Bon viatge!*

An unusual shop packed with
kitsch, practical, funny or zany
gadgets, including sheepskin
photo frames, fluorescent shower
curtains and genuine leatherette
sofas. Definitely just for fun.

# DECORATION, TABLEWARE AND DESIGN

Barcelona is reputed for being at the forefront of innovative contemporary design, so capitalise on your weekend by acquiring a designer piece for your home. If you have very eclectic tastes, you won't be disappointed by what's on offer – colonial, country, high-tech, kitsch, utility, unusual or surrealist – as many styles as there are shops.

## Molsa

**Plaça San Josep Oriol, 1 (C3)**
**☎ 93 302 31 03**
**Metro Liceu**
**Mon.-Sat. 10am-2pm, 4.15-8.15pm.**

At the foot of the Del Pi church steeple, Molsa has an authentic range of craft objects on display. – traditional ceramics from Galicia and Valencia, glassware from Majorca, blue-and-white-checked window boxes, reproductions of 18th-century Catalan tableware, sundials, and colourful *azulejos*.

## Beardsley

**Petritxol, 12 (C2/3)**
**☎ 93 301 05 76**
**Metro Liceu**
**9.30-1.30pm, 4.30-8pm.**

A shop window with an air of home-sweet-home about it, in this small lively street. Beardsley sells pot-pourri, dried flowers,

petit-point embroidery, needlework, white Girona porcelain, bathroom accessories and, in the basement, cardboard storage boxes (200-4,000 ptas) and personalised writing paper (595 ptas).

## Punto Luz

**Pau Claris, 146 (C1/2)**
**☎ 93 216 03 93**
**Metro Passeig de Gràcia**
**Mon.-Sat. 9.30am-1.30pm 4.30-8pm.**

No need to be kept in the dark, you'll find a sophisticated selection of lighting that will appeal to even the most demanding tastes. Say goodbye to those dreary old lampshades and dark colours. There are also lights and shades for the garden. Everything is bang up-to-the minute and fashionable.

## Dou Deu

**Doctor Dou, 10 (C2)**
**☎ 93 301 29 40**
**Tue.-Sat. 10am-2pm, 4.30-8.30pm.**

This shop, located not far from the MACBA in the Ravel district, has a good selection of limited-edition designer objects. From bedside lamps and handbags to bottle openers and fluorescent table mats, you can be sure of finding an original and reasonably-priced present here.

## Juan Soriano Raura

**Mayor de Gràcia, 53 (not on map)** ☎ 93 217 23 75
Mon.-Sat. 9am-1.30pm,
4.30-8pm.

When you leave the Passeig de Gràcia, make for this cut-price hardware shop. Dating from the 1890s, it's like an Aladdin's Cave full of amazing bric-a-brac. Every item comes with detailed instructions for use and you'll certainly find something you like amid the indescribable jumble that includes paella dishes, a small baking dish for *crema catalana* and *porronés* where you drink without letting the bottle touch your lips. A real curiosity shop.

## Coses de Casa

**Plaça San Josep Oriol, 5 (C3)**
☎ 93 302 73 28
**Metro Liceu**
Mon.-Sat. 10am-1.30pm,
4.30-8pm.

If you have a strong Catalan streak, then this is the place for you. Here in these antiquated surroundings you'll find a unique selection of Catalan fabrics, including the distinctive *llengos de Mallorca* in striking reds, blues and greens, with some promising materials in sunshine shades of golden yellow and coral pink.

## Entre Telas

**Plaça Vicenç Martorell, 1 (C2)**
☎ 93 317 76 14
Mon.-Sat. 10am-2pm,
5-8pm.

A textile workshop that has taken up lodgings under the arcades of a shady square in the Raval district, where two young designers happily produce a blend of craft and design. Hand-woven silk and cotton tinted with vegetable dyes are printed with exclusive, personalised designs. They're said to have 'good vibrations', so go ahead and buy.

## Caixa de Fang

**Freneria, 1 (C3)**
☎ 93 315 17 04
**Metro Jaume I**
Mon.-Sat. 10am-2pm,
4.30-8.30pm.

Behind the cathedral, foodies will find all the utensils they need to concoct tasty Catalan dishes – salamander irons (625 ptas),

ramekins for *crema catalana*, *porronés*, for drinking without letting your lips touch the bottle, olive-and-sand-coloured terracotta cooking pots, glazed ceramics and boxwood and olive-wood spoons (125 to 325 ptas).

## Servicio Estaciòn

**Arago, 270 (B/D2)**
☎ 93 216 02 12
**Metro Passeig de Gràcia**
Mon.-Fri. 9.30am-
2pm, 4.15-8pm,
Sat. 9.45am-2pm,
4.15-8.15pm.

A gigantic hardware shop, where you'll find waxed cloth and plastic and Formica kitchen tiles.

If you're looking for paella dishes (see p. 11), try Juan Soriano Faura (see p. 96).

## Taller de Lenceria

**Rosellon, 271 (C/D1)**
☎ 93 451 39 52
**Metro Diagonal**
Mon.-Sat. 10am-2pm, 4.30-8pm.

Elegant table and bed linen made to measure in cotton, linen and lace, plus a large selection of cotton piqué nightdresses and pyjamas you can have initialled.

## Sit Down

**Mallorca, 331 (A2)**
☎ 93 207 75 32
**Metro Verdaguer**
Mon.-Sat. 10am-1.30pm, 4.30-8pm.

You'll be spoilt for choice between re-issues of natural cane chairs by Oscar Tusquets and other designs by Joseph Hoffmann, Philippe Starck and Jose Luis Luscà, making use of colour and fabric and all reasonably priced (from 18,000 ptas).

## Tierra Extraña

**Rossellò, 226 (C/D1)**
☎ 93 487 95 88
Mon.-Sat. 10.30am-8.30pm.

As the name suggests, we're on foreign soil here, with Indonesian and colonial Indian furniture, parchment wall-lamps (13,000 ptas), small raffia bedside lamps, palm basket work and craft objects displayed on low rattan tables that will make you think you're in tropical climes.

## Pilma

**Diagonal, 403 (C/D1)**
☎ 93 416 13 99
**Metro Diagonal**
Mon.-Sat. 10am-2pm, 4.30-8.30pm.

Contemporary lifestyle in a transparent steel and glass setting. On the ground floor, kitchen and bathroom accessories, on the first floor a passageway leading to a loggia full of light, colourful furniture. From pure wool tartan plaids to futuristic baskets, by way of the Noguchi paper lantern, Pilma clearly has plenty to offer.

## Lulaky

**Consell de Cent, 333 (D2)**
☎ 93 488 00 50
Mon.-Sat. 9.30am-9pm.

A newly-opened combination of interior design and restaurant – you can have the place setting from your meal delivered to your door (2,200 ptas).

**LOVE AT FIRST SIGHT**

**ASPECTOS**
**Rec, 28 (D3)**
☎ 93 319 52 85
**Metro Jaume 1**
**Mon.-Fri. 4.30-8pm,**
**Sat. 10.30am-2pm.**

Interior designer Camilla Hamm's new gallery features up-and-coming young designers whose work is produced in limited editions. Come here to see some unusual pieces presented in elegant, sophisticated surroundings and find something just right for your home.

And there's nothing to stop you trying out the Catalan tea-cloths, four-wicked candles and coloured glasses as well. It's a new kind of take-away!

## Zeta

**C. d'Avinyò, 22 (C3)**
☎ 93 412 51 86
**Mon. afternoon-Sat. 11am-2pm, 5-9pm.**

Kitsch is back and you can find it at Zeta's. Or, if you prefer, there's a wide range of Peace and Love and other seventies-style items. Futons, artificial sunflowers, leopardskin lampshades, subdued lighting, plus that little bit of kitsch and of course bags of atmosphere. Friendly and amusing, and a shop not to miss.

## Otros Mundos

**Provenza, 330 (B/D1)**
☎ 93 458 60 17
**Metro Verdaguer**
**Mon. afternoon-Sat. 10am-2pm, 4.30-8.30pm.**

The atmosphere of this warehouse is irresistibly exotic, with beds hung with mosquito nets, colonial planter armchairs (68,000 ptas), Javanese teak chairs and bamboo chaises longues (78,000 ptas). With a bit of luck, they might even serve you a glass of punch. Whatever you do, don't forget to visit Barcelona's two design institutions: **BD** Mallorca, 291 ☎ 93 458 69 09 Metro Verdaguer Mon.-Sat. 10am-2pm, 4-8pm (see p. 25), and **Vinçon** Passeig de Gràcia, 96 ☎ 93 215 60 50 Mon.-Sat. 10am-2pm, 4.30-8.30pm. (see p. 50).

# ANTIQUE DEALERS, SECONDHAND SHOPS AND FLEA MARKETS

From the bric-a-brac of an antique dealer to the open-air secondhand stalls in the Plaça del Pi, you'll discover the pleasures of bargain-hunting in the sun. You may not find the bargain of the century, but don't let that stop you bringing back something small to remind you of Barcelona and the warm Mediterranean when you get back home.

Every Thursday from 9am-8pm (except in August), secondhand stalls set up shop in the cathedral square. Search hard and you may find some pretty *azulejos*, old ceramics, a doll with porcelain eyes, or carved sperm-whale teeth. Bric-a-brac with soul.

## Mercat Sant Antoni
**Comte d'Urgell, 1 (B2)**
☎ 93 423 42 87
**Metro Sant Antoni
Clothes Mon., Wed., Fri. and Sat. 9am-7pm, books Sun. 9am-2pm.**

In an iron and glass hall dating from 1872, Sant Antoni's market is a bargain-hunter's paradise, where ladies

## Els Encants
**Plaça de las Glòries (not on map)**
☎ 93 246 30 30
**Metro Glòries
Mon., Wed., Fri. and Sat. 9am-7pm in winter, 8am-8pm in summer.**

'Encant' comes from cantar (singing), as merchants used to sing out the prices. Els Encant is like a cross between a scrap metal dealer and a jumble sale. There are bicycle wheels, books, old leatherette sofas, buttons, lamps – you name it, somebody at Els Encant will be selling it, a real flea

market in the sun, but you will need to get there early for the best finds.

## El Bulevard dels Antiquaris
**Passeig de Gràcia, 55 (C1/2)**
☎ 93 215 44 99
**Metro Passeig de Gràcia
Mon.-Sat. 9.30am-8.30pm.**

In an elegant shopping centre in the Passeig, art lovers and collectors will find a clutch of good quality antique shops. It's a chance to take a quick look at a wide selection of quality items.

## Mercat Gotic
**Avinguda Catedral, 6 (C3)**
☎ 93 291 61 18
**Metro Liceu.**

who lunch happily rub shoulders with high-spirited teens, looking for clothes and accessories from eras before they were born. Every Sunday from 10am to 2pm, secondhand clothes change hands, and old editions of Tintin in Catalan, faded posters, colour prints and film magazines all vie for the favours of keen collectors. In one corner, they swap the latest characters from Japanese role playing games. There is something to suit all tastes here.

## La Inmaculada Concepcion

Rosselló, 271 (C/D1)
☎ 93 217 78 90
**Metro Diagonal**
Mon.-Sat. 10.30am-2pm,
4.30-8pm.

One of the pioneers of recycled furniture – *Modernista*, industrial and American-style office furniture – and also the designer of lamps with parchment lampshades.

## Gotham

C. Cervantes, 7 (C3)
☎ 93 412 46 47
Mon.-Sat. 10.30am-2pm,
5-8.30pm.

A shop decorated in acid colours and translucent sixties plastic, with fifties to seventies furniture to brighten up your world. Better than a course of vitamins and sure to banish the blues.

## BANYS NOUS AND PAJA

The Banys Nous and Paja streets (Metro Liceu), in the heart of the old town, are crammed with interesting shops. Enter the maze and wander around to your heart's content. Details of the opening times of some of the shops in the section 'From Antiques to Azulejos' in 'Antiques and Old Lace' (see p. 20) follow:

### Josep Pascual i Armengou

Banys Nous, 14 (C3)
☎ 93 301 53 65
Mon.-Sat. lunchtime
11am-1.30pm, 5-8pm.

### Erika Niedermaier

Paja, 11 (C3) ☎ 93 412 79 24
Mon.-Sat. lunchtime
10.15am-1.30pm, 4-8pm.

### Sant Yago

Paja, 8 (C3) ☎ 93 301 53 79
Mon.-Fri. 10.30am-1.30pm,
4.30-7pm.

### Maria Jose Royo

Banys Nous, 22 (C3)
☎ 93 302 35 20
Mon.-Fri.10am-1.30pm,
4.30-8pm, Sat. 11am-2pm.

# HOBBIES AND COLLECTIONS

You don't need to be particularly wealthy to be a collector, as long as you don't decide to collect Fabergé eggs that is, and some people do collect the strangest things. However, whatever your particular interest there's nothing quite like the pleasure of adding a foreign piece to your collection whilst on your travels.

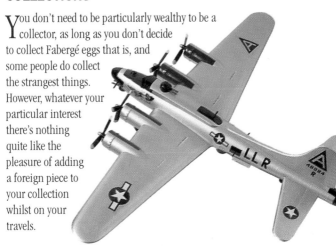

### A. Monge

Boters, 2 (C2)
☎ 93 317 94 35
Metro Liceu
9am-1.30pm,
4-8pm.

Philatelist or not, Monge is worth a visit for the *Modernista* shop front alone. Since 1904, Senor Monge has prided himself on his knowledge of coins and stamps. His collections include 1st and 2nd-century coins, and the more affordable sets of stamps of the Olympic Games (500 ptas).

### Palau

Pelai, 34 (C2) ☎ 93 317 36 78
Metro Catalunya
Mon.-Sat. 10am-1.30pm,
4-8.30pm.

A firm founded in 1935 selling the Scalextric, Meccano and Fleischmann brands. Everything is on a small scale here except the cashier and the prices. Expect to pay between 26,000 and 68,000 ptas for an electric train. Have a look at the dozens of miniature electric lights – they're just like the real thing.

### Jazz Collectors

Ptge Forasté, 4 bis
(not on map)
Ferrocarril Av. Tibidabo
Mon.-Sat. 10.30am-2pm,
4.30-8.30pm.

The Soley family's collection specialises in jazz. It comprises ten thousand or so titles which will be the envy of all jazz fans. Although the shop is dedicated to jazz, it also sways to the beat of Rhythm and Blues, salsa, tango etc.

### Norma Comics

Passeig de Sant Joan, 9
(D2)
☎ 93 245 45 26
Metro Arc de Triomf
10.30am-2pm,
5.30-8.30pm.

Comic book collectors find this a good source for first editions, while fans of role-playing games, war games and *Star Wars* aficionados can stock up on cards and dice. If none of these are of any interest to you, you can look at the Japanese printing machines, which are also for sale.

### L'ESTANC

**Via Laietana, 4 (C2/3)**
**☎ 93 310 10 34**
**Mon.-Fri. 8.30am-2pm,**
**4-8pm, Sat. 9am-2pm.**

If you are keen on good quality cigars you should visit this shop. The owner is a cigar *puros* (purist). He is an expert in Cuban tobacco and stocks over 150,000 cigars in his cellar. Connoisseurs keep theirs locked up and meet to discuss them with other aficionados from time to time. Comfortable chairs and a glass of whisky help the conversation to flow. A box of twenty-five No.4 Montecristo cigars costs around 13,000 ptas.

and a good source of material on foreign films too of course.

### Hobby Tècnic

**Comte d'Urgell, 182 (B1/2)**
**☎ 93 323 39 45**
**Mon.-Sat. 9.30am-1.30pm,**
**4.30-8.30pm.**

These models will occupy you on rainy days when you get back home. Hobby tecnic sells top international brands of model planes, boats and trains. A technical service is also available and there are also spare parts for sale.

### Mercado de Numismatica y Filatelia

**Plaça Reial (C3)**
**Metro Liceu.**

On Sunday mornings (9am-2.30pm) coin and stamp collectors gather beneath the arcades of the Plaça Reial. Regardless of whether you have a particular interest in coin and stamp collecting, this is a very colourful market and good value for a spot of simple people watching.

### Hobby Art Center

**Europa, 23 (not on map)**
**☎ 93 410 29 61**
**Metro Maria Cristina**
**Mon.-Sat. 9am-9pm.**

All the toys here are made in the old-fashioned way, including lead soldiers, trains and dolls with china faces. They'll please young and old alike, from those nostalgic for the games of their childhood, to today's children discovering them for the very first time.

### Groucho y Yo

**Aragòn, 359**
**(B/D2)**
**☎ 93 458 35 91**
**Metro Verdaguer**
**Mon.-Sat. morn.**
**10.30am-2pm,**
**5-8pm.**

This shop specialises in everything to do with the cinema. It has posters, film stills, postcards and books. So if you are a film buff this will be paradise

# THE ART MARKET AND ART GALLERIES

The most important art galleries are situated in Consell de Cent street (between Pau Claris and Balmes), while newly fashionable areas , such as the Raval or Born, are witnessing the opening of new galleries spearheading the avant-garde. We suggest a few places, both legendary and visionary, to whet your appetite.

### Sala Parès
**Petritxol, 5 (C2/3)**
**☎ 93 318 70 08**
**Metro Liceu**
**Mon.-Sat. 10.30am-2pm,**
**4.30-8.30pm,**
**Sun. 11am-2pm.**

The oldest art gallery in the city (1840), where the work of the great turn-of-the-century Catalan painters, such as Rusinol, Casas, Nonell and Picasso, was exhibited. Each Sunday morning after attending mass, people would visit this avant-garde institution to discuss art, politics and religion. In 1928, Dali honoured it with his presence. A visit to this legendary place is essential for art lovers.

### Galeria Maragall
**Rambla de Catalunya, 116 (C1/2)**
**☎ 93 218 29 60**
**Mon.-Sat. 10am-1.30pm,**
**4.30-8.30pm.**

This gallery exhibits work by Catalan artists, in particular Tàpies, Miró and Barceló from the older generation of artists and Castro, Enrick and Carmé Bassa from the younger. This is also a good place if you are interested in lithographs. They have a very good collection and the prices aren't out of the question, starting at around 3,500 ptas.

### Metronom
**Fusina, 9 (D3)**
**☎ 93 268 42 98**
**Metro Jaume I**
**Tue.-Sat. 10am-2pm,**
**4.30-8.30pm.**

This is the gallery of the famous collector Rafael Tous, which flourishes in the shadow of the Born market. It also houses a contemporary art foundation which is one of the keystones of cultural life in Barcelona.

## Cultural Centre of the Caixa-Palau Macaya Foundation

**Passeig de Sant Joan, 108 (D1/2)**
**☎ 902 22 30 40**
**Tue.-Sat. 11am-8pm,**
**Sun. 11am-3pm.**

La Caixa is the fifth-largest non-profit making cultural institution in the world, hence its dynamism (see inset). Located in this remarkable *Modernista* palace, designed by Puig i Cadafalch, it has exhibition rooms, concert halls, reading rooms, sound archives, a video library, book-shop and bar.

## Editiones T

**Consell de Cent, 282 (D2)**
**☎ 93 487 64 02**
**Metro Passeig de Gràcia**
**Tue.-Sat. 10.30am-2pm,**
**5-8pm.**

Inaugurated in September 1994 by the son of Antoni Tàpies (see p.27), this gallery specialises in original graphic works, books illustrated by artists such as Arroyo, Campano, Chullida, Le Witt and, of course, Tàpies.

## Dels Angels

**Dels Angels, 16 (C2)**
**☎ 93 412 54 54**
**Metro Catalunya**
**Tue.-Sat. noon-2pm,**
**5-8.30pm.**

Galleries flourish in the restored area of the Raval, thanks to the opening of the Museum of Contemporary Art. This helps young experimental artists to become established. A drawing by Santi Moix, for example, will cost around 45,000 ptas, while paintings range from 150,000 to 520,000 ptas. A good place to come to spot new trends..

## Carles Poy

**Doctor Dou, 10 (C2)**
**☎ 93 412 59 45**
**Metro Catalunya**
**Mon.-Fri. noon-8pm, Sat.**
**10am-8pm, Sun. 10am-3pm.**

Behind the Museum of Contemporary Art, the owner of the gallery, Carles Poy, puts on exhibitions of promising young talent, such as Miquel Mont (from 50,000 ptas for a drawing, to 500,000 ptas for a painting), and Tony Grau (from 80,000 ptas for a carved wooden sculpture). There are also poetry readings and book presentations.

## LA CAIXA, NOT JUST A SAVINGS BANK

Since 1990, La Caixa (pronounce the Catalan 'x' like the English 'sh') has become the second most powerful banking body in Spain. Omnipresent in the Arts and Sciences, it has revived the turn-of-the-century tradition of patronage. Its five-pointed blue star logo designed by Miró, hovers over the whole city, a symbol of the economic and cultural power of Catalonia.

# CRAFT AND ECOLOGY

In Barcelona, as in many of the big cities of the world, people are hankering after returning to a simpler way of life. In keeping with this you can now buy *organicas*, shirts made from Peruvian cotton, and *tortillas paisanas*, made of wheat. If you are into a 'green' lifestyle, you can pursue it in Barcelona just as well as in London or New York.

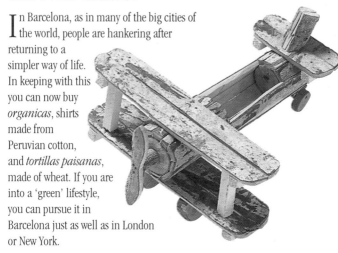

### Hôma

**Rec, 20**
**☎ 93 315 27 55**
**Metro Jaume 1**
**Tue.-Fri. 5-9pm,**
**Sat. 11am-2pm, 5-9pm.**

A former coffee warehouse in the Ribera has been converted into a very pleasant exhibition hall, with bedside lamps and exclusive eco-friendly wall lights in the primitive style, made of natural materials – raffia, wood and bamboo. The furniture by Ruben Vidal will add a 'recycled' touch to your home.

### Indian

**Pasaje Mercader, 16 (not on map) ☎ 93 487 37 03**
**Metro Verdaguer**
**Mon.-Sat. 10.30am-2pm,**
**5-8.30pm.**

Faience, delicate *azulejo* patterns created in the time-honoured way, embroidery and handmade carpets, traditional fabrics, Indian rice measures and colonial furniture. Those who particularly appreciate a blend of cultures should come to Indian.

### Arunachala

**Jovellanos, 1 (C2)**
**☎ 93 317 80 23**
**Metro Catalunya**
**Mon.-Fri. 9.30am-2.30pm,**
**4.30-8.30pm,**
**Sat. 10am-2pm, 5-8pm.**

This bookshop, a short walk from the Plaça de Catalunya specialises in the mysteries of the occult sciences, from Zen Buddhism to reincarnation and the New Age. There is a heady smell of incense on the air, which may encourage you to have your palm read and find out about your love life.

### Dauer

**Tallers, 48 bis (C2)**
**☎ 93 318 22 41**
**Metro Catalunya**
**Mon.-Sat. 10am-1.30pm,**
**4.30-8.30pm.**

The walls are lined with aquariums full of fish swimming up and down, as fish do. This shop specialises in piranhas, sea horses and other marine and freshwater creatures. Pay a visit if you are

feeling a bit stressed by the bustle of the streets outside and see if watching the fish will have the required calming effect. Its a bit tricky to take a fish home with you, but if you feel so inclined, they begin at 150 ptas.

## The Living Stone

**Petritxol, 3 (C2/3)**
**☎ 93 318 35 67**
**Metro Liceu**
**Mon.-Sat. 10am-2pm,**
**4.30-8pm.**

The Nordic name hides a sun-filled shop selling a range of eco-friendly, natural cosmetics perfumed with the scents of the Spanish countryside and the Orient. Bergamot, musk, honey, jasmine and patchouli await release from colourful glass bottles (500-2,500 ptas).

## Cereria Subirà

**Baixada Llibreteria, 7 (C3)**
**☎ 93 315 26 06**
**Metro Jaume I**
**Mon.-Sat. morning**
**9.30am-1.30pm,**
**4-7.30pm.**

In 1909, one of the city's oldest firms of candlemakers moved into this building built in 1847. Gilded panelling, two caryatids and an elegant staircase give it a timeless feel. Salvador Dali often used to come here, drawn by the old-fashioned atmosphere. The owner of Cereria Subirá is understandably proud of his hand-finished, natural beeswax candles costing around 150-2,000 ptas.

## Herbolari Antiga Casa Guarro

**Xuclà, 23 (C2)**
**☎ 93 301 14 44**
**Metro Catalunya**
**Mon.-Fri. 9am-2pm, 4-8pm,**
**Sat. 9am-2pm, 5-8pm.**

If conventional medicines are no longer having the required effect on your ailments, you can rediscover some age-old herbal remedies here. Also visit the natural products fair In the Plaça de Saint Josep, the first Friday and Saturday of every month.

# BOOKSHOPS AND OFFICE ACCESSORIES

Spanish people read the least number of books per head of all the countries in Europe. Yet Barcelona is traditionally associated with novels and art book publishing and the city has five monuments dedicated to books, which are given as gifts on Sant Jordi's Day (see p. 15). Perhaps this might get the people reading?

## Estilografica

Fontanella, 17,
☎ 93 318 64 95
Metro Catalunya
Mon.-Sat.
9am-1.30pm, 4-8pm.

Founded in 1938, this shop has a fine selection of pens, biros and pen holders, *unica en precios y calidad*, as well as a workshop for repairs. Despite email, letter writing lives on.

## Papirum

Baixada de la Llibreteria, 2 (C3)
Metro Jaume I
Mon.-Sat. 10am-2pm, 4.30 to 8.30pm.

A small shop lit by a porcelain lamp, it contains some fine local craft objects – seals, boxes, diaries and hand-made paper, lined with iridescent marbled paper. These items are made by Papirum and are absolutely unique in the city, from 500 to 7000 ptas.

## Continuarà

Via Laietana, 29 (C2/3)
☎ 93 310 43 52
Metro Jaume I
Mon.-Sat. 10.30am-3pm, 4-9pm.

Two floors that are home to every kind of comic strip book you can imagine. The first floor is devoted to the more modern heroes, while the one below is devoted to the old favourites such as Zorro, Spiderman and Superman, who, despite being eighty years old, are just as agile as ever.

## Llibreria del Raval

Carrer d'Elisabets, 6 (C2)
☎ 93 317 02 93
Metro Catalunya
Mon.-Sat. 10am-9pm.

This bookshop is located in the sanctuary of a former chapel, behind the new Museum of Contemporary Art. It resembles a vast library on whose shelves you can find almost anything and everything from large format art books, comic strip books and novels to more esoteric works.

## José Caballero

**Plaça de la Llana, 10 (D3)**
☎ 93 268 45 70
**Metro Jaume I**
**Mon.-Sat. 10am-8pm.**

If you're in the area of Santa Maria del Mar, do try this shop. There are old cinema posters, reviews from the turn of the century, faded postcards and children's comics that will take you back to your childhood. And if José isn't there, you'll find him on Sunday morning at Sant Antoni's market. (Comte d'Urgell,1 -B2- Metro Sant Antoni, every Sunday 10am-2pm).

## Tarlatana

**Comtessa de Sobradiel, 2 (C3)**
☎ 93 310 36 25
**Metro Jaume I**
**Mon.-Fri. 9am-7pm .**

In the Barrio Gòtico, Jaume Salvadó has perfected the art of bookbinding and framing in the traditional way. The workshop

upstairs is worth looking round. Tarlatana also has a selection of pens, diaries, blotters and coloured paper.

## Llibreria Rodes

**Carrer dels Banys Nous, 8 (C3)**
☎ 93 318 13 89
**Mon.-Fri. 10am-2pm, 5-8pm.**

The tone is set as soon as you cross the threshold. From floor to ceiling,the walls are lined with old works, out-of-print books and 18th-century engravings. There is a cat purring happily in the corner and the atmosphere is calm and hushed. Entirely fitting for such a bookshop set in the antiques district.

## Llibreria Sant Jordi

**Ferran, 41 (C3)**
☎ 93 301 18 41
**Metro Jaume I**
**Mon.-Sat. 9.30am-2pm, 4.30-9pm.**

Father and son have run this bookshop since 1880. The *Modernista* decor, with ivory woodwork, belongs to a bygone age. A warm welcome and knowledgeable help guide you in your choice of works on architecture, design and art. Just out of curiosity, take a look at the charming *calendari dels*

## BOOK AND MAGAZINE PUBLISHING

Barcelona is really the centre of the publishing industry in Spain and the bulk of the printers, paper mills and publishers are to be found in and around the city. It is therefore no coincidence that Barcelona gave birth to a number of publications, magazines and comic strip books, the latter being very much part of a non English-speaking European tradition.

*pagesos*, an astronomical and religious calendar, littered with nursery rhymes and sayings (500 ptas).

# GASTRONOMY

However you style yourself, gourmet, Epicurean, bon viveur, or just plain foodie, there is a great deal of scope for trying out new flavours in Barcelona and lots of opportunities to take some of these regional specialities home with you. Here are a few specialist shops to try.

### Colmado Quilez
Rambla de Catalunya, 63 (C1/2)
☎ 93 215 23 56
Mon.-Sat. 9am-2pm, 4.30-8.30pm.

A traditional grocer's that has offered a wide choice of high-quality local products for the past fifty years. Liqueurs, tinned foods and heady wines are piled from floor to ceiling in a chaotic, old-fashioned but charming way.

### Fargas
Plaça Cucurulla, 2 (C2)
☎ 93 302 03 42
Metro Catalunya
Mon.-Sat. 9am-1.30pm, 4-8pm.

A stone's throw from the cathedral, the pretty shop front of this

confectioner's promises old-fashioned delicacies. They're still made the traditional way, using a millstone to produce powdered drinking chocolate. Among the specialities of the shop are *bombons de tardor, catanis* – almond, caramel and chocolate sweets which are around 5,400 ptas per kilo.

### Comme-Bio
Via Laietana, 28 (C2/3)
☎ 93 319 89 68
Mon.-Sun. 9am-11pm.

As you may gather from the name, the products on sale at Comme-Bio exude well-being and health. They sell camomile, marjoram, thyme, passion-flower, organic chocolate, wholemeal bread and beer. There is nothing special about the setting, but you can also try the organic products on the premises.

### Caelum
Carrer de la Palla, 8 (C3)
☎ 93 302 69 93
Mon. aft.-Sun. morn.
10am-2pm, 5-8.30pm.

A new and highly unusual addition to the antique district. *Caelum* advertises 'monastery delights and temptations. An old-fashioned shop which boasts medieval recipes, communion wine and rose-petal jam. All these delicacies are prepared in secret within the confines of the

### TURRÓN, BLENDING FLAVOURS FROM NORTH AFRICA

The *turrón de Jijona* is an Arab sweet that's said to date back to the 15th century. Originally from North Africa, it's a subtle blend of Mediterranean flavours – almond, honey and cinnamon. It used to be sold during the three months of the Christmas *ferias*, but in 1850 these fairs ceased to be held and so the *turrón* vendors had to sell on the street instead, where you'll still find them today.

monasteries. You can try out these particularly holy specialities in a cellar occupying a former 14th-century public baths and also admire bed linen embroidered by nuns.

### Planelles-Donat

Portal de l'Angel, 7 and 25 (C2)
☎ 93 317 34 39
Metro Catalunya
Mon.-Sat. 10am-2pm, 4-8pm
Curcurulla, 9 (C2)
Mon.-Sat. 10am-2pm, 4-8pm,
Sun. 10am-2.30pm.

Five generations of the Donat family have been selling all kinds of *turrónes* (see inset) in slabs and also by weight to passers-by in the street. The windswept stall gets packed at Christmas time, when the people of Barcelona come to treat themselves. *Turrón* makes an ideal, typically Catalan present.

### J. Mùrria

Roger de Lluria, 85 (D1/2)
☎ 93 215 57 89
Metro Passeig de Gràcia
Mon.-Sat. 10am-2pm, 5-9pm.

All your senses will have a field day when you visit J. Murria. Everything is displayed in an exceptionally well-preserved *Modernista* setting. Haunches of Guijuelo ham, nuts, extra virgin olive oil, jams and preserves from Penedès – all extremely tasty treats for the sensitive palate.

### La Viniteca

Agullers, 7 (C3)
☎ 93 268 32 27
Metro Jaume I
Mon.-Sat. 8am-3pm, 5-9pm.

La Viniteca overflows with full-bodied red wines (Rioja 495 ptas), fruity dry white wines (Penedès 595 ptas), local sparkling wines (Cava Codorniu brut 995 ptas), rosés, spirits, etc.

### La Colmena

Plaça de l'Angel, 12 (C2)
☎ 93 315 13 56
Metro Jaume I
Mon.-Sun. 9am-9pm.

One of the few cake shops specialising in sweets and soft caramels flavoured with eucalyptus, pine, thyme, fennel and coffee (1,200 ptas/kg/2.2lbs). Since the start of the century, this sweet-shop has sold nougat with crème brûlée (*de biema*), *panellets* in marzipan on

All Saints' Day, and sweets to hungry people of all ages.

# Nightlife
## Practicalities

The designer Mariscal coined the following Catalan pun: 'Bar-cel-ona', i.e. Bar = bar, cel = sky, and ona = wave. This goes to show how inseparable the city is from its bars — the temples of a nightly ceremony performed just about everywhere. From cocktail lounges to legendary jazz bars, from post-modern decor to disused hangars, you can listen and dance to every conceivable rhythm. Be prepared to be intoxicated by it all and you too will thrill to the night.

## WHERE AND WHEN?

Barcelona nightlife is constantly changing. Trendy places are quickly replaced by new names, and cafes and bars succeed each other at an alarming rate. The people of Barcelona love going out, all age groups, all night and all year round. Its very difficult to recommend one district more than another because the hot spots vary according to the season. Thursday, Friday and Saturday nights are most popular. In summer, *carpas* (marquees) are erected in the port or stadiums, or even in the city heights. Always spectacular, they have the best bars of the season, and are definitely not to be missed.

## HOW TO GET AROUND

Use taxis to get from place to place – they're affordable and available in vast numbers. The city is generally safe, except for the Barrio Chino (Chinatown), an area notorious for drugs and prostitution. Take a taxi if you go there after dark.

## How much?

It is quite usual to only pay for your own drinks, which makes it possible to move from place to place without seriously damaging your budget. If you have to pay to get into a club the price usually varies between 1,000 and 2,000 ptas, but the first drink is often free, or the person accompanying you may get in free. Cinema tickets are cheap (around 700 ptas whereas theatre tickets are around 2,000 ptas.

## Some dos and don'ts

Don't set off too early – most places are dead before 11pm. It's also wise not to turn up at some of the discos until 2am, otherwise you're likely to be the only person there! If the partying goes on until dawn, there'll always be a bar to serve you *chocolate con churros* or a baker's to cut up a crispy *pa de coca* to keep you going. By then, you'll have discovered that Barcelona rarely sleeps. The life of the hard-working, hard-playing Catalan can be yours, provided you can keep up with it.

## How to make reservations

If you want to make a last-minute booking for a concert or show, your hotel porter will help you, but you'll need to have an idea of what you want to see or you may end up saddled with his choice. You can get information from *la Guia del Ocio*, and the *El Pais* and *la Vanguardia* newspapers, which will give you the prices and times of performances and the telephone numbers for bookings. For some shows, a 50% reduction is available three hours before the start of the performance. Enquire at the Tourist Information Office in the Plaça de Catalunya. Concerts at the Palau de la Musica are often very popular and seats need to be booked well in advance. As for the Liceu opera house, it has just been rebuilt after burning down for the third time in 1994.

## The Barcelona look

The discos and night clubs have no specific dress code, so you can wear what you like and if you're really partial to wigs and silk stockings, no-one will take offence. Barcelona is much less straight-laced and conventional than Madrid, so don't take too many smart clothes along for the evenings – concerts are really the only opportunities to dress up a little. As for restaurants, the atmosphere everywhere is very relaxed.

## *Tapas* bars and late snacks

### L'Arquer

**Gran via de les Corts Catalanes, 454 (B2)**
**☎ 93 423 99 08**
**Metro Rocafort**
**Every day**
**7pm-3am.**

*Tapas, copas y flechas*, or how to pass an evening playing at Robin Hood! Four Olympic archery ranges (1,200 ptas for half an hour) allow you to demonstrate your amazing skill, while nonchalantly sipping a 'm a g i c - p o t i o n' cocktail.

### La Bolsa

**Tuset, 17 (C1)**
**☎ 93 202 26 35**
**Metro Diagonal**
**Every day 6.30pm-3am.**

This bar has an unusual system, it is set up to work like the stockmarket. Drinks are quoted like commodities and the prices which are displayed on screens, fluctuate according to the amount consumed. An attractive brick and wood-panelled setting for whisky and vodka in a bull market.

### Zig Zag

**Plató, 13**
**(not on map)**
**☎ 93 201 62 07**
**Every day**
**10pm-3am.**

A classic bar that's been a favourite with the young people of Barcelona for twenty-one years. *Zig Zag*'s regulars opt for this happening place playing mainly jazz, funk and hip hop. Estrella and Ingrid will offer you a margarita or a pina colada, so why not sip on a cocktail, sit back and relax?

### Schilling

**Carrer Ferran, 23 (C3)**
**☎ 93 317 67 87**
**Every day 11-2am.**

Not far from the cathedral and newly opened, this is currently the 'in' place. An old knife factory has been turned into a café that has become very popular. Exposed stonework, subdued lighting and bistrot tables make a very cosy setting for a cosmopolitan and gay clientèle. Try to get here around 8pm.

### Replay Café

**Passeig de Gràcia, 60 (C1/2)**
**☎ 93 467 72 24**
**Mon.-Sun.**
**restaurant 1-4pm, 8.30pm-2am,**
***tapas* bar all day.**

Step into the hallway of this *Modernista* building and you'll be dazzled by the luxury of the decor. This is the place to come for some refreshment when you're out shopping. It's a combination of shop and restaurant that you'll want to visit more out of curiosity than for the cuisine.

### The Quiet Man

**Marqués Barbera, 11 (C3)**
**☎ 93 412 12 19**
**Every day 6pm-2.30am.**

Feeling nostalgic for an old Irish pub? Don't worry, even in Barcelona you'll be able to drink a pint of foaming Guinness or a pure malt whisky in an Irish setting, with Celtic music at the weekend. Olé !

### La Bodega Vasconya

**Gignàs, 13 (not on map)**
**Every day except Sun.**
**9am-1.30pm, 5.30-11pm.**

Miguel, manager and home distiller, proudly presents tapas to eat at the bar and liqueurs with lilting names – *Hidalgo de Chinchon*, *Moscatella* and *Barecha* – and generous and fruity flavours.

## Casa Fernandez

Santalo, 46 (not on map)
☎ 93 201 93 08
Metro Diagonal
Every day 1pm-1.30am.

If you suddenly feel hungry in the course of your night-time wanderings, go to Casa Fernandez for a quick bite and sample a selection of cold sausages and hams or a creamy *tortilla* washed down with the local Penedès wine. You'll soon be ready for more!

## El Tonell

Gignàs, 10
(not on map)
Tue.-Sun. 6pm-2am

This wine bar opened in 1923 in the Mercé district sells cider from the Asturias, heady Riojà wines accompanied by a selection of cold sausages and hams (*chorizo a la cidra* or *cabrales*, the local Roquefort). Bistrot chairs, and a colourful *azulejo* frieze await hungry night owls before they go to bed.

## El Salon

L'hostal d'en Sol, 6 (C3)
☎ 93 315 21 59
Metro Jaume I
Mon.-Sat. 1pm-3am.

El Salon is a friendly bar opening onto a little street behind the post office. Its cheerful blend of odd chairs and tables, Baroque chandeliers, exposed stonework and a comfortable old sofa that

make this an ideal setting for homemade pastries or a nice bowl of vegetable soup until as late as 3am.

## Canodrom Pavellò

Carrer de Llançà, 2 (not on map) ☎ 93 325 46 08
Metro Espanya
Every day 5-9pm.

You come here more for the atmosphere than the decor. On the Plaça d'Espanya greyhound track, gamblers stand at the bar and open the betting on the races. With its faded decor, this is a curiosity of the city. For those who enjoy the unusual and non-trendy 'local colour'.

## Escribà

Litoral Mar, 42
(not on map)
☎ 93 221 07 29
Tue.-Sun. 1.30-4.30pm,
Fri.-Sat. 8.30-11pm.

Since 1906 Escribà has specialised in home-made sweets and pastries – praline-flavoured chocolates and bitter chocolate cream slices – washed down with a cup of Ethiopian coffee. In this *chiringuito* (seaside restaurant) there are plenty of mouthwatering dishes for you to try.

### Un coche menys

Esparteria, 3 (D3)
☎ 93 268 21 05
Sat.-Sun. setting off at 10am, returning at 12.30pm (2,000 ptas), Tue. and Sat. setting off at 8.30pm, returning at midnight (5,000 ptas).

How to explore the city,. stay fit and help protect the environment. On Tuesday and Saturday evenings dozens of people set off on bikes in pursuit of a guide, criss-crossing the city in all directions. Aperitif and dinner are included and afterwards there's dancing. It's a good, easy way to get to know the Catalans and a few unusual places. All you need is a passport and the right sportswear.

## Late bars and all-night bars

### Velodrom

Muntaner, 213 (C1/2)
☎ 93 430 60 22
Metro Hospital Clinic
Mon.-Sat.. 6-2am.

From night to morning this forties bar attracts a cosmopolitan clientele. Time has blackened the walls and patinated the furniture, but the back room is a haven for billiard fans all night long. Bags of atmosphere.

### Nick Havanna

Rossello, 208 (C/D1)
☎ 93 215 65 91
Metro Diagonal
Sun.-Thu. 11pm-4am,
Fri.-Sat. until 5am.

Nick likes to boast that this is 'the ultimate bar'. In any case, it has live music on Thursdays, salsa and samba classes on Tuesdays, a Catalan book vending machine, if you feel like trying to read, and a pendulum describing the movements of the earth, all in a designer décor. If you like trendy places, this is for you.

### Le Marsella

Sant Pau, 65 (C3)
Metro Liceu
Mon.-Thu. 9pm-2.30am,
Fri.-Sun. 6pm-2.30am.

Located in the Raval district (beware of pickpockets), Indiana Jones would feel quite at home in this bar. Its original décor, old mirrors, bistrot chairs and marble tables create quite a nostalgic atmosphere. At the weekends a fortune teller will read cards for you.

### LONDON BAR

Nou de la Rambla, 34
☎ 93 318 52 61
Metro Liceu
Tue.-Sun. 7pm-4am.

The Raval district (beware of pickpockets) has fortunately preserved this bar, which opened in 1910 and where Picasso used to come on his nightly wanderings. The decor with the patina of time, tobacco smoke and jazz rhythms are reminders of the former Bohemian lifestyle. On some evenings, a trapeze artist whirls through the air in memory of the artists of the Barcelonés circus, which was destroyed during the Civil War.

### Snooker

Roger de Lluria, 42 (D1/2)
☎ 93 317 97 60
Metro Urquinaona
Every day 6pm-3am.

A splendid red and gold decor, with subdued alabaster lighting, Riart armchairs dotted here and there, and, as you might imagine a number of snooker players. A stylish setting for a mojito or Hawaiian cocktail.

## Zsa-Zsa

**Rossellò, 156 (C/D1)**
**☎ 93 453 85 66**
**Metro Diagonal**
**Mon.-Sat. 9pm-3am.**

The kilim covered walls are a blaze of colour, and together with the studied lighting and pale birchwood partition the décor is quite special. You can sip a cocktail at the bar on tall metal stools and the strains of salsa complete the atmosphere.

## Dot

**Nou de Sant Francesc, 7 (C3).**

Currently one of the best places, with a great DJ and film shows on the dance floor. A trendy place you shouldn't miss that's full to bursting every weekend. *Buenas copas et muchas risas*.

## Insolit

**Maremagnum, local 111 (C3)**
**☎ 93 225 81 78**
**Metro Barceloneta**
**Mon.-Sun. 2-11pm.**

With its futuristic decor, the latest cyber café is an Internet bar for late nights on the web. Half an hour's connection to Tokyo, Sydney or Slocombe-on-the-Mud costs 600 ptas.

## Tres Torres

**Via Augusta, 300**
**(not on map)**
**☎ 93 205 16 08**
**Mon.-Sat. 5pm-3am**
**Funicular Tres Torres.**

This beautifully preserved *Modernista* villa is a favourite haunt of the trendy young set. In summer, the terraces and garden turn it into a magical place, with little tables set out under the palm trees surrounded by bamboo armchairs. The ideal place to sip a glass of punch in the moonlight.

## LA FIRA

**Provenza, 171 (B/D1)**
**Metro Hospital Clinic**
**Mon.-Thu. 1pm-midnight,**
**Fri.-Sun. 1pm-5am.**

One of our favourite places. If you're nostalgic for the atmosphere of *La Strada*, you'll love the La Fira bar. An enthusiast brought the bric-a-brac of a disused fun-fair here piece by piece – distorting mirrors, arcade machines, a fortune teller, trapezes and roundabouts, all with a tale to tell. For those who love poetry in motion.

## Almirall

**Joaquin Costa, 33 (C2)**
**☎ 93 302 41 26**
**Metro Liceu**
**Every day 8pm-2am.**

Only a short walk from the Museum of Contemporary Art, this bar in the Raval has kept its original, pleasant *Modernista* setting. Local regulars congregate round the little bistrot tables or sit on the battered sofas.

## Mirablau

**Final, Avinguda de Tibidabo
(not on map)
☎ 93 418 58 79
At the foot of the funicular
Every day 11-5am.**

This bar with panoramic view is a must to round off a romantic evening. From 2am onwards, couples gather on the terrace and vow their love as they gaze at the city twinkling in the distance. A timeless classic.

## Partycular

**Avinguda de Tibidabo, 61
(not on map)
☎ 93 211 62 61
Every day from 7pm.**

A *torre* and villa with a romantic seaside decor high in the city hills. Order a cava under the palm trees before doing a tour of the property.

## El Born

**Passeig del Born, 26 (D3)
☎ 93 319 57 11
Metro Jaume I
Every day until 2am.**

The Plaça del Born has become the place for anyone wishing to spend a night on the town. A tour of the bars is a must, with the Miramelindo, El Born and El Copetin all vying for the favours of those intent on a night of pleasure. You can dance, sample some cocktails and set the world to rights until the wee small hours, if you have the stamina.

## Rosebud

**Adria Margarit, 27 (not on map), Avinguda de Tibidabo
☎ 93 418 88 85
Every day until dawn.**

Rosebud takes its name from the last word uttered by the hero of *Citizen Kane* and isn't a reference to the swimming pool and luxuriant garden. However, it's still an ideal place to come on a mild summer evening, when the enormous glass dome makes a pleasant setting.

## Gimlet

**Rec, 24 (D3)**
☎ 93 310 10 27
Every day 7pm-3am.

Back in the 70s Gimlet put new life into cocktails. The 50s-inspired decor, with its display cabinets, pays discreet homage to the Shaker style. Connoisseurs know they serve the best dry Martinis in the city here. Cocktail lovers take note.

## Torres de Avila

**Marquès de Comillas (A2)**
☎ 93 424 93 09
Metro Espanya
Thu.-Sat.
11pm-5am.

Talented designers have converted the two towers of the entrance to the Pueblo Espanol. Bars, billiard rooms and terraces decorated with stars by Mariscal are arranged on several levels like a set of Russian dolls. The panoramic view from the rooftop terraces is a must in summer.

## Palau Dalmases

**Montcada, 20 (D3)**
☎ 93 310 06 73
Tue.-Sat. 8pm-2am,
Sun. 8-10pm.

A sumptuous Baroque setting in an aristocratic palace on the Montcada, a stone's throw from the Picasso Museum. Gleaming mirrors, the scent of musk, amber and iris, bowls of fresh fruit and garlands of flowers bathed in candlelight turn the weekly concert of Baroque music into a dream.

## Cabarets, jazz, and shows

### La Boite

**Diagonal, 477 (C/D1)**
☎ 93 419 59 50
Every day 11pm-5.30am.

The best jazz cellar in the city, with a seventies decor and knowledgeable audience, presents legendary artists such as Lou Benett, Dr Feelgood and jazz musicians from all over the world, as well as bands playing funk-jazz, hard-soul, reggae, blues, etc. After the concert, the fevered atmosphere of the disco takes over.

### La Tierra

**Aribau, 230 (C1/2)**
☎ 93 414 27 78
Thu.-Sat. 11pm-5am.

Smart and clean but beginning to show its age, this is one of Barcelona's more trendy places, with something for every musical taste. Take your pick from salsa, rumba, funk, acid-jazz, swing country, New Orleans and blues.

## Tarantos

**Plaça Reial, 17 (C3)**
☎ 93 318 30 67
Shows Mon.-Sat. at 10pm
Entry charge 3,800 ptas.

The flamenco isn't popular with Catalans, but it you want to see this Andalusian dance during your stay then los Tarantos are the unrivalled masters of the art. Their singing and guitar playing and the artistry of the dancers make a wonderful show.

## Jamboree

**Plaça Reial, 17 (C3)**
☎ 93 301 75 64
Every day 9pm-5am.

Housed beneath the vaults of a former convent, the first jazz club opened in Spain, in 1959, has long since swapped the cornet for the saxophone, and blues, Dixieland, and New-Orleans jazz have made way for the pulsating rhythms of funk.

## LA BODEGA BOHEMIA

**Lancaster, 2 (C3)**
☎ 93 302 50 61
Every day 11pm-3am.

*Donde nacen los artistas* the sign outside boldly declares, but with Rosa from Granada vocalising, Valentin the supple Catalan sketching a few dance steps and syrupy Juan José singing 'Lola Lolita' as he has for the past twenty-five years, what chance *'A Star is Born'*? Two or three old dears in the audience respond with weak applause but you'll have the place more or less to yourself. A touching performance for tender hearts and sensitive souls.

# El Molino

**Vilà i Vilà, 99 (B3)**
**☎ 93 441 63 83**
**Metro Parallel**
**Shows every day except Mon.**

At the turn of the century, the Parallel became the haunt of the city's revellers, reminiscent, in its heyday, of Pigalle. El Molino is a survivor of the past, an old-fashioned music-hall with a rather seedy atmosphere. A variety of acts – cabaret singers circus acts and striptease artists – perform to the applause of a local audience seated on wooden chairs. A museum piece.

Phallic symbols, erotic reliefs and interesting sculptures set the scene of this place with a vengeance. The décor paying homage to Pedro Almodovar, the famous Spanish film director, has a provocative edge, as has the clientele, which includes a mixture of gays and straights. There is no admission charge, but it is pretty busy at the weekends.

## Nightclubs and discos

# Universal

**Maria Cubi, 182 (B1)**
**☎ 93 201 35 96**
**Mon.-Sat. 11pm-4.30am.**

Opened in 1985 this is still the trendiest place in Barcelona, but beware of the decibel level. This is a classic bar with designer décor. There are always queues to get in, but they are quite choosey about whom they will admit.

# Satanassa

**Arribau, 27 (C1/2)**
**☎ 93 451 00 52**
**Metro Universitat**
**Every day 8pm-5am.**

# Otto Zutz

**Lincoln, 15 (not on map)**
**☎ 93 238 07 22**
**Tue.-Sat. from midnight.**

Situated in an old warehouse there are six bars and an enormous dance floor on three levels. The policy on the door is to vet hopeful entrants, you will only get in if they like the look of you. An interesting mix of people, from football stars to artists and designers. Live bands sometimes play here.

# Antilla Cosmopolita

**Muntaner, 244 (C1/2)**
**☎ 93 200 77 14**
**Metro Hospital Clinic**
**Every day 10.30pm-5am.**

Every night talented musicians churn out the rhythms of Mambo, biguine, bachata and dambala. You may not know what they are, but the rhythm will soon get to you and you'll be up on the dance floor.

# Up and Down

**Numancia, 179 (not on map)**
**☎ 93 205 51 94**
**Tue.-Sat. from midnight.**

The place to come if you're with your parents – upstairs for them and downstairs for you. It's how the Barcelona middle classes solve the generation gap. Everyone under the same roof but each to his own quarters. Wear a tie and dine to music upstairs, or wear what you like and drink Coca-Cola downstairs.

# Luz de Gas

**Muntaner, 246 (C1/2)**
**☎ 93 209 77 11.**

The former Belle Epoque theatre has been turned into an enormous dance and concert hall, with the upper gallery a pleasant place for a quiet chat or tasty *bocadillo* ( Spanish-style sandwich). Clientele aged 7 to 77.

## Bikini

**Deu I mata, 105 (B1)**
☎ **93 322 00 05**
**Tue.-Sun. from 11.30pm.**

Situated under the Illa centre, 1,200m²/13,000sqft of floor space on two levels houses a concert hall, a dance floor and a calm lounge for quiet conversation. After falling into decline, this legendary Barcelona nightspot has risen from the ashes more vibrant than ever.

### Music

## Zeleste

**Almogavers, 122 (not on map)** ☎ **93 309 12 04**
**Fri.-Sun. until 5am.**

Beyond the Olympic Village, Zeleste has found a home in the apocalyptic setting of an industrial warehouse, the Poble Nou. According to what's on the programme, you'll hear folk music or hip hop in a hangar, while two small discos play grunge, rock, etc. next door. Pink patent Doc Martens and rocker jackets are needed to get in.

## Palau de la Musica

**Sant Francesc de Paula, 2 (C2)**
☎ **93 268 00 00/**
**93 317 10 96**
**Metro Urquinaona.**

If you're a classical music lover, find out what's on at this magnificent concert hall as soon as you arrive in the city. The splendid *Modernista* decor by Domenech i

## La Paloma

**Carrer Tigre, 27**
☎ **93 301 68 97**
**Thu.-Sun. evenings.**

A legendary dance hall with the charm of yesteryear that's well worth a visit. Everything is worthy of classification as a historical monument here, from the smooth crooners of the orchestra with their greying slicked-back hair to the stucco ornamentation of the balconies.

Montaner is also worthy of close attention (see p. 38, Ribera).

### Places not to miss in the Barrio de Gràcia

We recommend a tour of one of the city's most popular districts, but little known to tourists, the Barrio de Gracia. Spared by the rebuilding for the Olympics, it retains much of its original charm. A former suburb of little houses and gardens it has preserved its character thanks to its squares, covered markets, cafés and the Lliure theatre. Leave the metro at Metro Fontana and follow our guide, beginning with:

## Sol Soler

**Plaça del Sol, 13 (C1)**
☎ **93 217 44 40**
**Mon.-Fri. 6pm-2am,**
**Sat.-Sun. 1pm-2am.**

On the Plaça del Sol, there are at least half a dozen bars occupying the terraces. To start the evening, you can try mouth-watering *tapas* – chicken wings in sweet and sour sauce, tabouleh with fresh herbs, and vegetable and fish pâté. Bistrot tables, checkered tiles, and whirring fans set the scene for tasty food and local wines.

## Tons

**Xiquets de Valls, 14
(not on map)
☎ 93 237 78 20
Mon.-Sat. 10am-2pm,
5-8.30pm.**

This is an inspirational place for those who are interested in interior decoration. They sell lights, lampshades and doorknobs in original shapes and colours. If you want to try your hand at some decorative painting there are paints, brushes and stencils. They also have an interesting line of table linen.

## Café del Sol

**Plaça del Sol, 16
☎ 93 415 56 63
Every day until 3am.**

Sit on the terrace of the bar to see what's going on in the square – old people gossiping and taking a walk in their slippers, children playing ball and young couples smooching happily on the benches.

## Zoona libre

**La Perla, 26
Every evening except Sun.**

A photo of Bob Marley pinned to the wall looks down over the room. This is a reggae bar, with a rasta waiter and heady drinks. Paintings of the African jungle are for sale, adding an exotic touch.

## Bodega Manolo

**Torrente de las Flores,
101 (D1)
☎ 93 284 43 77
Lunch Tue.-Sat.,
dinner Thu.-Sat.**

A truly authentic, traditional *bodega*, where you sit at a neon-lit bar to drink the local wine, unless you happen to have brought along a bottle to fill from one of the barrels. If you have time, sit down and eat a snack of grilled green asparagus, tuna carpaccio and grilled cuttlefish with mushrooms. With checked tablecloths and the locals all around you, it's a slice of Barcelona life to savour to the full.

## Sabor Cubano

**Francesc Giner, 32
☎ 93 217 35 41
Every day 9pm-3am.**

A warm welcome and you feel just as if you've landed in the Caribbean. On Wednesday evenings, a live orchestra invites you to step into the spotlight and salsa. All the flavour of the West Indies right here in the Gràcia.

### LLIURE THEATRE

**Montseny, 47
(not on map)
☎ 93 218 92 51
Metro Fontana
Every day except Mon.**

Since 1976, this former cooperative has been home to the prestigious 'Free Theatre', with performances strictly in Catalan. If *A Midsummer Night's Dream* in Catalan doesn't tempt you, get round the language barrier by opting instead to see a performance of contemporary dance.

## Fronda

**Verdi, 15 ☎ 93 415 20 55
Every day except Tue.
7.30pm-3am.**

Close to the Verdi cinema, one of the few places to show films in the original language, Fronda takes care of its appearance, with a mahogany bar, subdued lighting, rattan armchairs and tables, a relaxed atmosphere and a jazz accompaniment.

# More handy words and phrases

Castilian Spanish is widely spoken in Barcelona although Catalan is probably slightly more prevalent. Spanish is certainly easier to pronounce, but be aware that you will see Catalan on menus, signs etc. Our Handy Words and Phrases are in Castilian Spanish (see also back flap of the cover).

## USEFUL EXPRESSIONS

**Good morning**
buenos días

**Good afternoon**
Buenas tardes

**Good evening**
Buenas noches

**Can you speak more slowly, please?**
¿Puede hablar mas despacio, por favor?

**Do you understand?**
¿Me entiende?

**I am sorry**
Lo siento/ Disculpe

**Is it possible...?**
¿Sería posible....?

**I want...**
Quiero...

**How?**
¿Cómo?

**What is your name?**
¿Como se llama?

**My name is ...**
Me llamo ...

**Free (no charge)**
Gratis

**Toilets/wc**
Baño or aseos

**No smoking**
No fumar

**Here/there**
Aqui/allá

**Early**
Temprano

**Late**
Tarde

**Slow**
Lento

**Fast**
Rápido

**Another**
Otra vez

**Before**
Antes

**After**
Dopo

**During**
Durante

**Near**
Cerca

**Now**
Ahora

**Up there**
Arriba

## AT THE HOTEL

**Do you have any rooms?**
¿Tiene habitaciónes?

**Hotel**
Hotel

**Bed & breakfast**
Pensión

**With a double bed**
Con cama doble

**With twin beds**
Con dos camas

**With a balcony**
Con balcón

**Full board**
Pensión completa

**Is breakfast included?**
¿Está incluído el desayuno?

**We are leaving tomorrow**
Nos vamos mañana

**At what time can you...?**
¿A qué hora es posible...?

## IN THE RESTAURANT

**Meal**
Comida

**The wine list**
La lista de vinos

**What is the dish of the day?**
¿Cual es el plato del dia?

**What is the house specialty?**
¿Cual es la especialidad de la casa?

**Tip**
Propina

**Plate**
Plato

## DRINKS

**Still/sparkling**
Sin gas/con gas

**Red/white**
Tinto/blanco

**Sparkling wine**
Cava

**Sherry**
Jerez

**Lemonade**
Limonada

**Orange juice**
Zumo de naranja

**Tea**
Té

## SUNDRIES

**Sugar**
Azúcar

**Salt**
Sal

**Pepper**
Pimienta

**Mustard**
Mostaza

**Sauce**
Salsa

**Spicy**
Picante

**Oil**
Aceite

**Vinegar**
Vinagre

**Sandwich**
Bocadillo
**Omelette**
Tortilla
**Egg**
Huevo
**Rice**
Arroz
**Fruit**
Fruta

MEAT AND FISH
**Meat**
Carne
**Ham**
Jamón
**Sausage**
Chorizo/embutido
**Blood sausage**
Morcilla
**Shrimp**
Langostino/gamba
**Squid**
Pulpo
**Oysters**
Ostras

NUMBERS
**1** uno
**2** dos
**3** tres
**4** cuatro
**5** cinco
**6** seis
**7** siete
**8** ocho
**9** nueve
**10** diez
**11** once
**12** doce
**13** trece
**14** catorce
**15** quince
**16** dieciseis
**17** diecisiete
**18** dieciocho
**19** diecinueve
**20** veinte
**21** veintiuno
**22** veintidos
**30** treinta
**40** cuarenta

**50** cincuenta
**60** sesenta
**70** setenta
**80** ochenta
**90** noventa
**100** cien
**1,000** mil
**2,000** dosmil
**5,000** cincomil
**1,000,000** un millon
**first**
primero/a
**second**
segundo/a
**third**
tercero/a
**fourth**
cuarto/a
**fifth**
quinto/a

TIMES AND DATES
**Yesterday**
Ayer
**Today**
Hoy
**Tomorrow**
Mañana
**One minute**
Un minuto
**One hour**
Una hora
**Half an hour**
Media hora
**Quarter of an hour**
Cuarto de hora
**It is midnight**
Es medianoche
**It's noon**
Es mediodia
**It's one o'clock**
Es la una
**See you tomorrow**
Hasta mañana
**What time is it?**
¿Qué hora es?
**Watch**
Reloj

DAYS OF THE WEEK
**Monday**
Lunes

**Tuesday**
Martes
**Wednesday**
Miércoles
**Thursday**
Jueves
**Friday**
Viernes
**Saturday**
Sábado
**Sunday**
Domingo

MONTHS OF THE YEAR
**January**
Enero
**February**
Febrero
**March**
Marzo
**April**
Abril
**May**
Mayo
**June**
Junio
**July**
Julio
**August**
Agosto
**September**
Septiembre
**October**
Octubre
**November**
Noviembre
**December**
Diciembre

IN THE TOWN
**News-stand**
Kiosco de revistas
**Bookshop**
Librería
**What time does it open/close?**
¿A qué hora abre/cierra?
**Straight on**
Todo recto
**Right/left**
Derecha/izquierda

**At the end of**
Al final de

**Next to**
Al lado de

**Opposite**
Frente a

**Up/down**
Arriba/abajo

**Above/below**
Sobre/debajo

**Entrance**
Entrada

**Exit**
Salida

**I would like to go**
Quisiera ir

**Timetable**
Horario

**By plane/train/car**
Por avión/tren/coche

**Airport**
Aeropuerto

**Do I need to change?**
¿Debo cambiar de platforma?

**What platform does it leave from?**
¿De qué plataforma sale?

**Bicycle**
Bicicleta

**On foot**
A pie

**Bend**
Vuelta

## SHOPPING

**Size**
Talla

**Small**
Pequeña

**Medium**
Mediana

**Large**
Grande

**Bigger**
Más grande

**Smaller**
Más pequeño

**In another colour**
De otro color

**It's too expensive**
Es demasiado caro

**Big/little**
Grande/pequeño

**Money**
Dinero

**Price**
Precio

**I would like to buy**
Quisiera comprar

**Where can I find...?**
¿Dónde puedo encontrar...?

**Sale goods**
Rebajas

**Secondhand objects**
Objetos usados/de segunda mano

**Bag**
Bolsa

**Belt**
Cinturón

**Book**
Libro

**Boots**
Bota

**Cap**
Gorra

**Cotton**
Algodón

**Dress**
Vestido

**Fashion**
Moda

**Gold**
Oro

**Hat**
Sombrero

**Stamp**
Sello

**Jacket (for men)**
Americana

**Jacket (for women)**
Chaqueta

**Leather**
Piel

**Linen**
lLino

**Lingerie**
Lencerìá

**Raincoat**
Iimpermeable

**Serviettes**
Servilleta

**Shirt**
Camisa

**Shoes**
Zapatos

**Shop**
Tienda

**Silk**
Seda

**Silver**
Plata

**Size**
Medida

**Skirt**
Falda

**Socks**
Calzetina

**Square**
Cuadro

**Tablecloth**
Mantel

**Tie**
Corbata

**Toy**
Juguete

**Wool**
Lana

## MAKING A PHONE CALL

**Phonecard**
Tarjeta telefónica

**Do you have a phone?**
¿Tiene un teléfono?

**Can I leave a message?**
¿Puedo dejar un mensaje?

**Could you speak up, please?**
¿Puede hablar más alto, por favor?

**Could you speak more slowly?**
¿Puede hablar mas lento?

**Wait a moment, please**
Espere un momento, por favor

## AT CUSTOMS

**Customs officer**
Advanero

**Identity card**
Carta de identidad

**Nothing to declare**
¿Nada a declarar?

**Passport**
Pasaporte

**Personal objects**
Objetos personales

# Conversion tables for clothes shopping

## Women's sizes

### Shirts/dresses

| U.K | U.S.A | EUROPE |
|-----|-------|--------|
| 8 | 6 | 36 |
| 10 | 8 | 38 |
| 12 | 10 | 40 |
| 14 | 12 | 42 |
| 16 | 14 | 44 |
| 18 | 16 | 46 |

### Sweaters

| U.K | U.S.A | EUROPE |
|-----|-------|--------|
| 8 | 6 | 44 |
| 10 | 8 | 46 |
| 12 | 10 | 48 |
| 14 | 12 | 50 |
| 16 | 14 | 52 |

### Shoes

| U.K | U.S.A | EUROPE |
|-----|-------|--------|
| 3 | 5 | 36 |
| 4 | 6 | 37 |
| 5 | 7 | 38 |
| 6 | 8 | 39 |
| 7 | 9 | 40 |
| 8 | 10 | 41 |

## Men's sizes

### Shirts

| U.K | U.S.A | EUROPE |
|-----|-------|--------|
| 14 | 14 | 36 |
| $14^{1}/_{2}$ | $14^{1}/_{2}$ | 37 |
| 15 | 15 | 38 |
| $15^{1}/_{2}$ | $15^{1}/_{2}$ | 39 |
| 16 | 16 | 41 |
| $16^{1}/_{2}$ | $16^{1}/_{2}$ | 42 |
| 17 | 17 | 43 |
| $17^{1}/_{2}$ | $17^{1}/_{2}$ | 44 |
| 18 | 18 | 46 |

### Suits

| U.K | U.S.A | EUROPE |
|-----|-------|--------|
| 36 | 36 | 46 |
| 38 | 38 | 48 |
| 40 | 40 | 50 |
| 42 | 42 | 52 |
| 44 | 44 | 54 |
| 46 | 46 | 56 |

### Shoes

| U.K | U.S.A | EUROPE |
|-----|-------|--------|
| 6 | 8 | 39 |
| 7 | 9 | 40 |
| 8 | 10 | 41 |
| 9 | 10.5 | 42 |
| 10 | 11 | 43 |
| 11 | 12 | 44 |
| 12 | 13 | 45 |

### More useful conversions

| 1 centimetre | 0.39 inches | 1 inch | 2.54 centimetres |
|--------------|-------------|--------|------------------|
| 1 metre | 1.09 yards | 1 yard | 0.91 metres |
| 1 kilometre | 0.62 miles | 1 mile | 1. 61 kilometres |
| 1 litre | 1.76 pints | 1 pint | 0.57 litres |
| 1 gram | 0.35 ounces | 1 ounce | 28.35 grams |
| 1 kilogram | 2.2 pounds | 1 pound | 0.45 kilograms |

This guide was written by **Marie-Ange Demory** with the collaboration
of **Marie Barbelet, Isabelle Bénéteau** and **Aurélie Joiris**
Translated by **Christine Bainbridge**
Project manager and copy editor **Margaret Rocques**
Series editor **Liz Coghill**
Additional research and assistance: Georgina Hawkes and Christine Bell

We have done our best to ensure the accuracy of the information contained in this guide.
However, addresses, phone numbers, opening times etc. inevitably do change from time
to time, so if you find a discrepancy please do let us know. You can contact us at:
hachetteuk@orionbooks.co.uk or write to us at Hachette UK, address below.

Hachette UK guides provide independent advice. The authors and compilers do not accept any
remuneration for the inclusion of any addresses in these guides.

Please note that we cannot accept any responsibility for any loss, injury or inconvenience
sustained by anyone as a result of any information or advice contained in this guide.

#### Photo acknowledgements

*Inside pages:* **Laurent Parrault** : pp. 2, 3 (c.c.), 10 (t.r., b.l.), 11, 12 (t.r., c.r., b.r.), 13 (c.l.), 14, 15, 16 (t.l., b.l.), 17 (t.l.), 18, 19, 20, 21, 22 (b.c., r.), 23 (b.l., b.r., c.r.), 24 (t.r.), 25 (c.l., b.c.), 26 (t.r. J. Miró © ADAGP, Paris 1997 , c.l.), 27 (t.r., c.l., b.c.), 28 (t.r., b.l.), 29 (t.l., b.l.), 35, 36, 37 (t.r.), 39 (c.l.), 40 (b.l., b.r.), 41 (t.c., b.r.), 42 (b.l., b.r.), 43 (t.l., c.), 44 (t.r.), 45 (c.l., b.r., b.l.), 46 (b.l.), 47 (c.r., b.r.) 48, 49 (c.), 50 (t.r., t.l., t.c., c.r.), 51, 52 (c.r.), 53 (b.r., t.l., t.c.), 54, 55, 56, 57 (t.l., t.r., c., b.r.), 58 (b.l.), 59 (t.l., t.r.), 60 (c., b.l.), 61 (t.l., c., b.l., b.r.), 62, 63 (b.r.), 64 (t.r., b.l.), 65 (t.l.) J. Miró © ADAGP, Paris 1997 , b.l., 67 (t.l., b.c.), 74 (b.l.), 76 (t.l.), 77, 78, 79 (c.r.), 84 (t.r., b.r.), 86 (b.l. , c.), 87, 88, 89, 90 (t.r., b.r.), 91 (t.r., t.l., t.c.), 92 (t.r.), 93 (b.r., b.l.), 94, 95, 96 (t.r.), 98, 99 (c.), 100 (t.c., b.r.), 101 (b.r.), 102 (t.r., b.r.), 104, 105 (b.c.), 106 (t.r., b.l.), 107 (t.l.), 108, 109 (t.l., c.r.), 110 (t.r., c.l. , b.l.), 111 (t.l., c.r., b.r.), 114 (t.l., b.l.), 115, 116 (t.l.), 117 (t.l., t.r., c.r.), 118 (c.l., b.r.), 119 (t.l., b.r.), 120 (t. l.), 121, 122; **Christian Sarramon** : pp. 3 (b.l.), 10 (c.r.), 12 (c.l.), 13 (t.l., c.r.), 16 (t.r.), 17 (b.r.), 22 (c.l.), 23 (t.c.), 24 (b.l., b.r.), 25 (t.l., b.r.), 27 (b.r. J. Miró © ADAGP, Paris 1997), 28 (c.r.), 29 (t.r.), 34, 37 (b.l., b.c., b.r.), 38 (c.l., b.r.), 39 (t.r.), 40 (c.), 42 (c.l.), 43 (b.r.), 44 (b.l.), 45 (t.r.), 46 (t.r., b.r.), 47 (t.l., b.l.), 49 (t.l.), 50 (c., b.l.), 52 (b.l.), 53 (c.r., b.l.), 57 (b.l.), 58 (t.r.), 59 (c.c., c.r., b.r.), 60 (b.r.), 61 (t. r.), 63 (t.r., c.c., c.l.), 64 (b.r.), 65 (t.r.), 66, 67 (c.c., b.r.), 76 (c.c.), 84 (c.r.), 85 (b.l., t.r.), 90 (b.l.), 91 (c., b.r.), 92 (b.l., b.c.), 96 (b.c.), 97 (b.l. , b.c.), 100 (b.l., c.r.), 101 (c.r. , c.l.), 102 (c.l.), 107 (b.l., b.r.), 111 (b.l.), 116 (b.), 117 (b.), 118 (t.r.), 119 (b.l.), 120 (c.r.); **Éric Guillot** : p. 96 (c.r.), p. 106 (c.); **Hachette Livre** : pp. 26 (b.r.) © Succession Picasso, Paris 1997 (DR), 38 (t.r.), 40 (t.r.) W. Kandinsky © ADAGP, Paris 1997; **C. Sarramon/Maison de Marie-Claire** : p. 16 (c. r.); **Ici et la** : p. 41 (b.l.); **Hôtel Arts Barcelona** : p. 70 (t.l.); **Hôtel Condes de Barcelona** : p. 70 (c.r.); **Hôtel Claris** : p. 70 (b.l.); **Hôtel Metropol** : p.71 (t.r.); **Hôtel Gran Derby** : p. 72 (c.l.); **Hôtel Montecarlo** : p. 72 (t.r.); **Hôtel Rivoli Ramblas** : p. 72 (b.l.); **Hôtel Romàntic** : p.73 (t.r., b.l.); **Reial Club Maritim** : p. 75 (b.l.). **La Balsa** : p. 75 (b.r.); **La Estrella Sitges** : p. 79 (b.r.); **Forum** : p. 84 (b.l.); **Groc** : p. 85 (t.l.); **Replay Store** : p. 86 (t.r.); **Bulevard Rosa** : p. 92 (c.r.); **L'Illà** : p. 93 (t.l.); **Entre Telas** : p. 97 (t.c.); **Otros Mundos** : p. 99 (t.l.); **BD** : p. 99 (b.r.); **Hobby Art Center** : p. 103 (t.l., b.r., t.c.); **Editiones T** : p. 105 (t.l.); **La Caixa** : p. 105(c.r.); **Cereria Subirà** : p. 107(c.r.); **Tarlatana** : p. 109 (b.); **Caelum** : p. 110 (b.d); **Replay Cafe** : p. 114 (t.r.).

*Front cover:* **Laurent Parrault** : t.l., t.r., c.l. J. Miró © ADAGP, Paris 1997, c.r., b.l., b.r.; **J.M. Foujols, Stock image** : t.c. premier plan; **C. Bouvier, Stock image** : c.r. (figure); **C. Maeder, Pix** : b.c. (figure); **Christian Sarramon** : c.c.
*Back cover:* **Laurent Parrault** : t.r., c.c. (figure); **Christian Sarramon** : c.l. , b.c.

**Illustrations** Pascal Garnier      **Cartography** © Hachette Tourisme

First published in the United Kingdom in 2000 by Hachette UK

© English Translation, revised and updated, Hachette UK 2000
© Hachette Livre (Hachette Tourisme) 1999

Distributed in the United States of America by Sterling Publishing Co., Inc.
387 Park Avenue South, New York, NY 10016-8810

A CIP catalogue for this book is available from the British Library

ISBN 1 84202 005 6

Hachette UK, Cassell & Co., The Orion Publishing Group, Wellington House, 125 Strand,
London WC2R 0BB

Printed and bound in Italy by Vincenzo Bona

If you're staying on and would like to try some new places, the following pages give you a wide choice of hotels, restaurants and bars, with addresses.

Although you can just turn up at a restaurant and have a meal (except in the most prestigious establishments), don't forget to book your hotel several days in advance (see p. 68). Enjoy your stay!

# STAYING ON
# A LITTLE LONGER

**P**lease note that prices given are a guide only and are subject to change.

## Barcelona

### Gran Hotel Catalonia★★★★★
C. Balmes, 142
☎ 93 415 90 90
Metro Diagonal.
*This hotel in a strategic setting near the Diagonal and Passeig de Gràcia is one of the most traditional in the city. With many years' experience behind it, it will please those who like old-fashioned service. It also has a car park.*

### Calderon★★★★
Rambla de Catalunya, 26
☎ 93 301 00 00
Metro Passeig de Gràcia.
*In a marvellous setting on the Rambla de Catalunya, a stone's throw from the city's most popular shops, the Calderon offers the practical comfort of designer rooms with parquet flooring. There are also 15 luxury suites.*

### Majestic★★★★
Pg de Gràcia, 70
☎ 93 488 17 17
Metro Passeig de Gràcia.
*This hotel in the stately Passeig de Gràcia is one of the city's classics. Recently renovated inside, it still has a turn-of-the-century façade and its reputation has remained intact.*

### Ambassador★★★★
C. Pintor Fortuny, 13
☎ 93 412 05 30
Metro Liceu.
*A stone's throw from the Ramblas and the Boqueria market in a typical Barcelona street, this hotel offers charming views, impeccable service and a swimming pool.*

### Gran Hotel Barcino
C. Jaume 1/6
☎ 93 302 20 12
Metro Jaume 1.
*If you're looking for a medium-sized hotel (53 rooms) offering 4-star service in the Barrio Gotico, then this is the place to come. Ask for a quiet room away from the noise of the street.*

### Balmes★★★
C. Mallorca, 216
☎ 93 451 19 14
Metro Passeig de Gràcia.
*If you're staying in the city in summer, this hotel has the enormous advantage of having a swimming pool and small garden. Around a hundred modern rooms and a supervised car park make it a practical place to stay.*

### Oriente★★★
La Rambla, 45
☎ 93 302 25 58
Metro Liceu.
*Within the 17th-century cloister of the St Bonaventura monastery, come here for its starry past, rather than for comfort. Antononi filmed here with Jack Nicholson, and Hemingway had his indispensable bottle of whisky at his elbow.*

### De l'Arc★★
La Rambla, 19
☎ 93 301 91 98
Metro Catalunya.
*Near Plaça de Catalunya, this neat little hotel with 45 rooms is both pleasant and practical. Good value for money and not to be missed.*

### Messon Castilla★★
C. Valdoncella
☎ 93 318 21 82
Metro Catalunya.
*In an alley in the Raval, a stone's throw from the Museum of Contemporary Art, this Spanish inn has made every effort to stay kitsch in a trendy district. 56 rooms with a rustic Castilian decor and a supervised car park.*

### Cortès★★
C. Santa Anna, 25
☎ 93 317 91 12
Metro Catalunya.
*This 45-room hotel offering a warm welcome and basic comfort is in the pedestrian area of Santa Anna. Quiet at night and lively in the daytime, it's ideal for exploring the city on foot.*

### Roma Reial★
Plaça Reial, 11
☎ 93 302 03 66
Metro Liceu.
*An inexpensive hotel in an imposing setting. From the 52 rooms with a view of the square you can watch the comings and goings of life in the Barrio Gòtico night and day. The Quinze Nits restaurant is close by and just as affordable (see p. 77).*

### Comercio★
C. Escudellers, 15
☎ 93 318 74 20
Metro Liceu.
*With the same owner as the Roma Reial, this inexpensive little hotel is impeccably clean and quiet. Well located in the old part of the city, it's perfect for people on a budget. The same is true of the La Fonda restaurant in the same street.*

**I**f you'd like to stay outside Barcelona, you'll find a choice of hotels in Sitges, Torrent and Aiguablava in the selection below.

## Sitges

### La Renaixença★★
Ila de Cuba, 13
☎ 93 894 83 75.
*If you want to spend your break in this idyllic little seaside resort (40km/25 miles from Barcelona), you can stay all year round at this Modernista villa with elegant, old-fashioned decoration and a charming turn-of-the-century atmosphere. Not to be missed.*

## San Agaro

### Hostal de la Gavina★★★★★
Pl. de la Rosaleda
☎ (00 34) 972 32 11 00.
*One of the finest luxury hotels on the Costa Brava, with antique furniture and old masters on the walls. Peace and quiet in a luxury setting are the order of the day, with tennis, a swimming pool, a sauna and excellent cuisine. Uninterrupted view of the sea. An hour and a quarter from Barcelona.*

## Torrent

### Mas de Torrent★★★★★
Finca Mas del Rei
☎ 00 34 972 30 32 92.

There are 30 suites decorated with contemporary paintings in this 18th-century farmhouse. A swimming pool and tennis courts, with horse riding and golf nearby, make a pleasant way to extend your weekend in Catalonia. 130km/80 miles north of Barcelona, near Bisbal.

## Aiguablava

**Aiguablava**\*\*\*\*
Platja de Fornells
17255 Begur
☎ (00 34) 972 62 20 58.
*Four successive generations have built the reputation of this hotel on the Costa Brava. Children's activities, volley-ball, a seawater swimming pool and direct access to the beach make it the ideal place for families. 150km/95 miles north of Barcelona, near Gerona.*

HOTELS

Generally speaking, the prices shown are for a complete meal, not including drinks. Please note that some places only take cash and that the prices are a guide only.

## Ribera

**La Floreta**
Plaça Olles, 4
☎ 93 268 13 84
Open Mon.-Sun.
*In a charming square, this restaurant serves delicious dishes in a scented setting. Lunch on goat's cheese salad and homemade tarts washed down with fruit juice.*

**Salero**
Carrer Rec, 60
☎ 93 319 80 22
Open Mon.-Sat.
*This former tuna-salting warehouse brings a breath of New York to the Santa Maria del Mar district. It naturally serves tuna tartare and Japanese-style dishes based on fresh vegetables. The set lunch is good value at 1,100 ptas.*

**La Flauta Magica**
Banys Vells, 18
☎ 93 268 44 94
Open Mon.-Sat.
*Next to the new weaving and silk painting workshops, this restaurant serving cocina natural is a must for the organically aware. The owner prides himself on serving the only antibiotic-free, organic beef in the city. And as his restaurant is one of the nicest, we'll take his word for it.*

**Hofmann**
Argenteria, 74
☎ 93 319 58 89
Closed Sat. and Sun.
*Originally a cookery school, Hofmann is now one of the best restaurants in the city. Come here to sample new Mediterranean cuisine by Mey Hofmann, who concocts delicious gourmet dishes. Around 6,000 ptas.*

## Raval

**Selenus**
Angels, 8
☎ 93 302 26 80

Open Mon.-Sat., closed Sun. and Mon. eve.
*Not far from the Museum of Contemporary Art and the ideal place to nourish body and soul after a morning spent studying abstract art. You can enjoy grilled salmon with fresh vegetables.*

## L'Eixample

**Mordisco**
Rossellon, 265
☎ 93 218 33 14
Open every day.
*With its practical setting a stone's throw from the Passeig de Gràcia, you come here more for a quick meal than a gourmet extravaganza. The mixed salad buffet and fast food menu are just right for this and the service is to match.*

**La Vaqueria**
Deu i Mata, 141
☎ 93 419 07 35
Open every day except Sat. and Sun. lunchtime.
*For fans of the rustic-style, this former barn has been stylishly renovated with carefully chosen bric-a-brac. Milk churns and bales of hay make you feel as if you are in a country and western film – appropriately enough since Vaqueria means cowshed. There is also a disco and a piano bar. The lunch menu features fish tartare and fresh market produce.*

**Lulaky**
Consell de Cent, 333
☎ 93 488 00 50
Open Mon.- Sat. lunchtime.
*This restaurant is in the basement of an interior designers. It is a perfect place to stop for lunch if you are shopping in the district. If you like the lunchtime tableware you can buy it on the first floor before you leave. Set meals at around 2,200 ptas.*

## Gràcia

**Botafumeiro**
Gran de Gràcia, 81
☎ 93 218 42 30
Open every day.
*A Barcelona seafood institution, with lobsters, crabs, sea spiders, Galician percebes and sea bass.*

*A very traditional decor but a very lively bar. Allow 8-10,000 ptas each.*

**Taberna del Cura**
Gran de Gràcia, 83
☎ 93 218 17 99
Open every day.
*A very rustic-style restaurant with exposed brickwork and hams hanging from the ceiling and strings of garlic and onions – and that's just the décor. The menu itself specialises in meat, with Catalan sausage, shoulder and rib of lamb that's grilled in front of you. À la carte meal at around 2,500 ptas.*

**Café Salambo**
Carrer Torrijos, 51
☎ 93 218 69 66
Open every day.
*A stone's throw from the Verdi, one of the few cinemas in the city to show films in the original language, this restaurant in the Gràcia (see p. 48) is very welcoming, with its subdued lighting, wooden seats and traditional stews. The owner tells endless stories about the district. Set lunch 1,300 ptas.*

**Mesopotamia**
Verdi, 65
☎ 93 237 15 63
Open Mon.-Sat.
*Don't miss this trendy new restaurant serving Iraqi cuisine – dolma, curries, vegetables in season and meat kebabs served on designer plates Gourmet set meal 2,500 ptas.*

**Envalira**
Planeta, 35
☎ 93 218 58 13
Open Tue.-Sat. for lunch and dinner, Sun. for lunch.
*Don't overlook this local restaurant with its regulars and traditional dishes – arroz a la marinera (rice), grilled cuttlefish, monkfish with prawns and cockles. An ordinary setting, but good food and a warm welcome. Set meal at around 2,500 ptas.*

## The city heights

**Can Cortada**
Avda de l'Estatut de Catalunya
☎ 93 427 23 15
Open every day.

*In summer, take advantage of the light breeze from the hills to sit on the terrace of this 11th-century farmhouse. The menu combines produce from the land and the sea, including chicken with prawns, Catalan-style cod with beans, and pig's trotters. Around 4,000 ptas. Come by taxi.*

### Vivanda
Major de Sarrià, 13
☎ 93 203 19 18
Open Tue.-Sat.
*Ideal in summer when you can take advantage of the lovely, shady terrace. Often full to bursting, with the 1,300 ptas set lunch attracting office workers from the area. Excellent value for money at lunchtime.*

## Barrio Gotico

### Culleretes
Carrer Quintana, 5
☎ 93 317 30 22
Open Tue.-Sat and Sun. lunchtime.
*This is the ideal place to celebrate a birthday, wedding anniversary or other special occasion. The waiters in white jackets are happy to give advice on what to order – they have been serving torrades with garlic and tomatoes and graellades for years and so know what they are talking about. Set lunch at 1,500 ptas.*

### Juicy Jones
Cardenal Casanas, 7
☎ 93 302 43 30
Open Tue.-Sun.
*The vegetarian set meal at 975 ptas varies every day. It's currently a good deal, so do make the most of it. The psychedelic decor and two waitresses who look as if they're just back from Katmandu are charming. You can come in simply to have a soya or fresh fruit milkshake and, as a bonus, have your cards read in the back room. A stone's throw from the Ramblas and the Plaça del Pi.*

### Café de l'Académia
Carrer Lledo, 1
☎ 93 319 82 53
Open Mon.-Fri., for breakfast as well.

*With its stone walls and exposed beams, subdued lighting and red glazed tiles, this is a very welcoming place. The menu is tempting, too, and you won't be able to resist the artichoke and parmesan soup, mushroom risotto and green asparagus salad (3,500 ptas). Enjoy!*

### Ateneu gastronomic
Pas de l'Ensenyança, 2 bis
☎ 93 302 11 98
Open Mon.-Sat. lunchtime.
*The regulars from the nearby Town Hall have made this their local. Colleagues who want to get to know one another gather round Mediterranean specialities, including dishes from Portugal, Aragon and Ampurda. It's a friendly, relaxing place, with a well-stocked cellar (enoteca) that loosens tongues and makes you want to stay on. Around 3,000 ptas.*

RESTAURANTS

# BARS

## Pas del Born
Calders, 8
☎ 93 319 50 73
Open every night.
*This bar in the trendy Born district (Ribera) is really more of a music-hall, with variety shows twice a month, flamenco singers and dancers every Friday, and, on Wednesdays and Saturdays, nonchalantly-swinging trapeze artists, who may invite you to dance.*

## Barroc Café Bar
Carrer Rec, 67
☎ 93 268 46 23
Open every night, 10pm-3am.
*The Barroc Café's distinctive coloured stucco creates a warm, intimate setting. There's a bohemian air about the place, with billiards, jazz and blues (twice a week) adding to the atmosphere and ensuring a pleasant evening.*

## La Vinya del Senyor
Plaça Santa Maria, 5
☎ 93 310 33 79
Open Tue.-Sun. noon-1am.
*A very pleasant terrace in one of the city's charming squares, where you can taste the local wines.*

## Café Kafka
Calle Fusina, 7
☎ 93 310 05 26
Open every night.
*This newly-converted warehouse a stone's throw from the Born market is reminiscent of New York. You have to come late, as with all the Born bars. You can have dinner first at the nearby and equally trendy Salero (see previous pages).*

## Hans Bar
Muntaner, 473
☎ 93 211 17 13
Closed Sun and Holy Week.
*This restaurant's regular clientèle tends to be quite bourgeois – regulars in the Born area tend to be a little younger and street-wise . The Hans turns into a bar from 1am onwards.*

## Glaciar
Plaça Reial, 3
☎ 93 302 11 63.
*An ideal meeting-place for those who start the nightly round of the bars in the older districts of the city. A vast terrace with a cosmopolitan and bohemian atmosphere.*

## Pipa Club
Plaça Reial 3, principal
☎ 93 302 47 32.
*A private club which is open to the public. It has a very British atmosphere with pipe-smokers in the sitting room, in keeping with the club's name. There are also occasional jazz and blues concerts.*

# DISCOS

## Jazzmatazz
Pje Domingo, 3
Open Wed.-Sat. 10pm-4am.
*All kinds of events take place here, including theatre and dance. This is a relatively new venue which provides live music most nights, including jazz, blues and funk.*

## Luna Mora
Marina, 19
☎ 93 221 61 61
Open Wed.-Sun. 10.30pm-5am.
*A recently-opened disco near the Arts Hotel in Port Olimpic. For the past two years, this has been one of the city's hottest nightspots, with disco music, 80s revival, and live broadcasts in a lunar-inspired decor.*

## Moog
Arc del Teatre, 3
☎ 93 318 59 66.
*In the space of a year, this place has become a must for techno fans. The clientèle is quite young on the whole and every Wednesday there is a visit from an internationally-known DJ. Very lively.*

## Dietrich
Consejo de Ciento, 255
☎ 93 451 77 07
Open 6pm-2.30am.

*A colourful café, disco and gay bar frequented by a sometimes provocative clientèle.*

## Lizard
Platon, 15
☎ 93 414 00 32.
*A popular music venue frequented by the sophisticated and fashionable, dancing to funk, hip hop and acid jazz, all mixed by talented DJ Angelo.*

## Made in Brasil
Consell de Cent, 384
☎ 93 265 25 26
Open every night, 8pm-2.30am.
*There is something in every corner of the place to remind you of Brazil. Toucans and parrots, fine sand and shells, the Brazilian flag and footballers' shirts, all accompanied by a samba, lambada or capoiera, you might almost think you were there.*

# BARS/CAFÉS

# A SHORT WALK IN THE BARRIO GÒTIC

Start from *Santa Maria del Mar*, a delightful church at the bottom of the c/de Montcada in the *Barrio Gòtic*. Continue up the c/de Montcada until you reach the beautiful medieval *Museu Picasso* on the right-hand side. A little further up the street you will come to the junction with the c/de la Princesa, turn left here and continue across *Plaça de l'Angel*. You are now on the c Jaume I, from where you turn right onto the c Freneria which will take you up to the cathedral. Pause here to look at the cathedral, or *La Seu*, as it is known. This is one of Spain's greatest Gothic buildings. Opposite you can see a frieze by Picasso portraying people dancing the *Sardanas*, the traditional Catalan dance. This is the heart of the *Barrio Gòtic* in the old town.

Cross the large square in front of the cathedral, the *Plaça Nova*, and head for the *Palau Episcopal* on the square's western side, This is the former bishop's Palace. You cannot go inside, but you can see the fine outer staircase. From the bishop's palace take the c/de la Palla until you reach the delightful *Plaça Sant Josep Oriol*, and stop for a drink at the *Bar del Pi*. At the weekend you may find the square given over to an artist's market

with street musicians and entertainers. If you don't fancy a drink at the bar here, try the adjacent *Plaça del Pi* where you can sip *horchata*, made from barley and typically Catalan. Take a look at the church of *Santa Maria del Pi*. Built in the 14th century, it was burned down in 1936, but restored in the 1960s. It is mainly gothic in style, but has a Romanesque door and some impressive stained glass windows inside.

From here continue along the c Cardenel Casanas which will take you to the Barrio's legendary street, *La Rambla.* Turn right and you will see the covered market *La Boqueria*, a little further up on the left. This is a must for all food lovers. Even if you don't buy any of the cheeses, hams, spices, nuts or dried fruit on sale, it is a real pleasure to see local produce well displayed and to gain an idea of the kinds of food Catalans eat every day.

Once leaving the market, turn right and walk back down *La Rambla* until you come to the *Gran Teatre del Liceu* on the right. It has had a troubled past. First built in 1847, then rebuilt after a fire in 1861, it was regarded as the finest opera house in Spain. However, in 1893 it was bombed by an Anarchist and destroyed again, killing twenty people at the same time. Finally, it was accidentally burned down once more in 1994. Now newly

restored again, keep your fingers crossed for its future in the new millenium.

Back on *La Rambla*, walk on a little further and turn right onto the c Nou de La Rambla. On the left-hand side you will see the *Palau Güell*, one of Gaudí's many buildings in the city. Don Eusebio Güell, Gaudí's most important patron, commissioned it in 1885. It is now a museum dedicated to Gaudí's and other *Modernista* architects' ideas. Most of Gaudí's buildings are still in private hands, so it is quite rare to be able to visit their interiors. You can remedy the situation therefore, by visiting this museum. The *Palau Güell* was the first modern building to be designated a world heritage site by UNESCO. When you leave the building, just glance across the street to number 6. This is where Picasso's studio was located in 1902 and from where he began his Blue Period. Incidentally, Picasso did not like Gaudí's work at all.

Walk back up the street to join *La Rambla* once more. This time, cross the road and take the c Colom, leading off *La Rambla* which takes you into *Plaça Reial*. This elegant square in the Italianate style was constructed around 1850 according to plans by Frances c Daniel Molina. It has iron street lamps by Gaudí and a fountain depicting the Three Graces at its centre. Rather down at heel and seedy at one time, the square was frequented by drug pushers, drunks and the general n'er-do-well, but was cleaned up in the 1980s. It still has its fair share of eccentrics and the odd dubious looking character, but it is a great place from which to watch people and, on the terraces of one of its cafés of bars, to relax after your walk.

# A SHORT WALK

# NOTES

NOTES

# INDEX FOR SHOPS

# INDEX OF BARS, CAFES & RESTAURANTS AND NIGHTLIFE VENUES

# HACHETTE TRAVEL GUIDES

Titles available in this series:

A GREAT WEEKEND IN PARIS  (ISBN: 1 84202 001 3)
A GREAT WEEKEND IN AMSTERDAM  (ISBN: 1 84202 002 1)
A GREAT WEEKEND IN ROME  (ISBN: 1 84202 003 X)
A GREAT WEEKEND IN NEW YORK  (ISBN: 1 84202 004 8)
A GREAT WEEKEND IN BARCELONA  (ISBN: 1 84202 005 6)
A GREAT WEEKEND IN PRAGUE  (ISBN: 1 84202 000 5)

*Also to be published in 2000*
A GREAT WEEKEND IN FLORENCE  (ISBN: 1 84202 010 2)
A GREAT WEEKEND IN LISBON  (ISBN: 1 84202 011 0)
A GREAT WEEKEND IN NAPLES  (ISBN: 1 84202 016 1)
A GREAT WEEKEND IN LONDON  (ISBN: 1 84202 013 7)
A GREAT WEEKEND IN BERLIN  (ISBN: 1 84202 061 7)
A GREAT WEEKEND IN BRUSSELS  (ISBN: 1 84202 017 X)
A GREAT WEEKEND IN VENICE  (ISBN: 1 84202 018 8)
A GREAT WEEKEND IN VIENNA  (ISBN: 1 84202 026 9)

## HACHETTE VACANCES
Who better to write about France than the French?
A series of colourful, information-packed, leisure and activity guides
for family holidays by French authors. Literally hundreds of suggestions
for things to do and sights to see per title.

*To be published in 2000*
PROVENCE & THE COTE D'AZUR  (ISBN: 1 84202 006 4)
BRITTANY  (ISBN: 1 84202 007 2)
LANGUEDOC-ROUSSILLON  (ISBN: 1 84202 008 0)
POITOU-CHARENTES  (ISBN: 1 84202 009 9)
SOUTH-WEST FRANCE  (ISBN: 1 84202 014 5)
PYRENEES & GASCONY  (ISBN: 1 84202 015 3)

## ROUTARD
Comprehensive and reliable guides offering insider advice for the
independent traveller.

*To be published from Summer 2000*
PARIS  (ISBN: 1 84202 027 7)
PROVENCE & THE COTE D'AZUR  (ISBN: 1 84202 019 6)
BRITTANY  (ISBN: 1 84202 020 X)
ANDALUCIA  (ISBN: 1 84202 028 5)
SOUTHERN ITALY, ROME & SICILY  (ISBN: 1 84202 021 8)
GREEK ISLANDS & ATHENS  (ISBN: 1 84202 023 4)
IRELAND  (ISBN: 1 84202 024 2)
CALIFORNIA, NEVADA & ARIZONA  (ISBN: 1 84202 025 0)
BELGIUM  (ISBN: 1 84202 022 6)
THAILAND  (ISBN: 1 84202 029 3)
CUBA  (ISBN: 1 84202 062 5)
WEST CANADA & ONTARIO  (ISBN: 1 84202 031 5)